Intermediate

Phonics Intervention Centers

Variant Consonant & Vowel Sounds

Writing: Camille Liscinsky
Content Editing: De Gibbs
Lisa Vitarisi Mathews
Copy Editing: Cathy Harber
Art Direction: Cheryl Puckett
Cover Design: Liliana Potigian
Illustrator: Matt Ward
Design/Production: Arynne Elfenbein
Kathy Kopp
Yuki Meyer
Marcia Smith

EMC 3528

Evan-Moor
EDUCATIONAL PUBLISHERS®
Helping Children Learn since 1979

Congratulations on your purchase of some of the finest teaching materials in the world.

Photocopying the pages in this book is permitted for <u>single-classroom use only.</u> Making photocopies for additional classes or schools is prohibited.

Contents

How to Use This Book

The centers in this book are designed to be completed in a small-group setting. All materials are included for groups of up to 6 students. The activities have been carefully crafted to meet the needs of students receiving Tier 2 Response to Intervention instruction, as well as the needs of any other students who are learning foundational phonics skills. The target skills in *Variant Consonant and Vowel Sounds* include recognizing the sounds of *r*-controlled vowels, diphthongs, and consonants with variant sounds and applying those sounds to read words.

For the Teacher

 **Lesson Plan** The skills in each unit are taught through teacher-led explicit instruction and are practiced through phonemic-awareness, hands-on, and written activities.

A fully scripted lesson plan cycles through auditory, oral, visual, and hands-on letter-sound activities that help students decode and read new words.

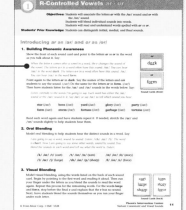

front　　　　*back*

Scaffolded activities help guide students through the lesson.

Sound Cards

Vocabulary cards feature target sounds and aid students in blending sounds to read words.

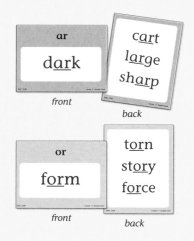

front　　*back*

Answer Keys

Each center includes a two-sided page of answer keys, showing mat activities on one side and written application activities on the other side.

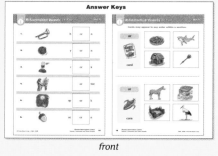

front

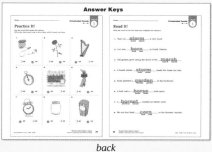

back

For the Student

Activity Mats and Task Cards

Each unit has six sets of activity mats and corresponding task cards, providing individual group members with their own materials for practicing the target skill.

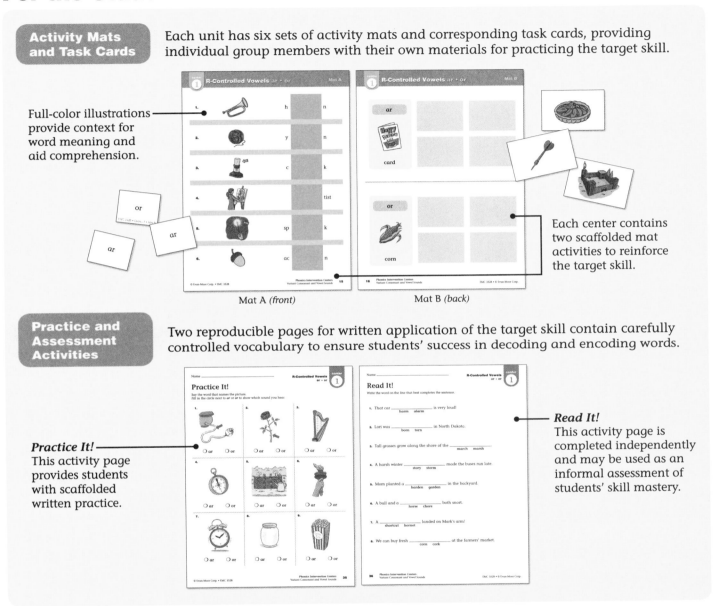

Full-color illustrations provide context for word meaning and aid comprehension.

Each center contains two scaffolded mat activities to reinforce the target skill.

Mat A *(front)*   Mat B *(back)*

Practice and Assessment Activities

Two reproducible pages for written application of the target skill contain carefully controlled vocabulary to ensure students' success in decoding and encoding words.

Practice It!
This activity page provides students with scaffolded written practice.

Read It!
This activity page is completed independently and may be used as an informal assessment of students' skill mastery.

Record Forms

Two reproducible record forms are included for tracking and assessing students' progress, individually or as a group. The *Group Progress Record* provides space for written comments and an assessment of skill mastery for each student in a particular group. The *Student Progress Record* includes a detailed breakdown of each center's objectives to informally assess an individual student's skill mastery.

How to Make and Store the Centers

You Will Need

- pocket-style folders (1 per center)
- business-size envelopes or small, self-locking plastic bags (12 per center)
- scissors, tape, marking pen
- laminating materials and equipment

Steps to Follow (for each center)

1. Remove the perforated pages and laminate all color pages. (Do not laminate the *Practice It!* and *Read It!* activities.)

2. Attach the cover page to the front of the folder.

3. Place the lesson plan in the left-hand pocket.

4. Cut apart the sound cards and the set of answer keys and place them with the lesson plan in the left-hand pocket of the folder.

5. Place all activity mats in the right-hand pocket.

6. Cut apart the task cards for Mat A and Mat B and sort them by student number (located on the back of most cards).

7. Keep each set of cards in a separate envelope or plastic bag and place them in the right-hand pocket of the folder.

8. Reproduce one copy of the *Practice It!* and *Read It!* activities for each student and place them in the right-hand pocket of the folder.

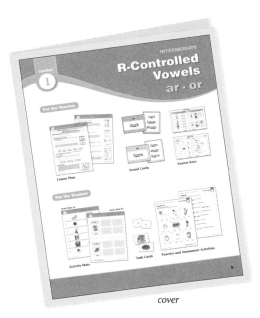

cover

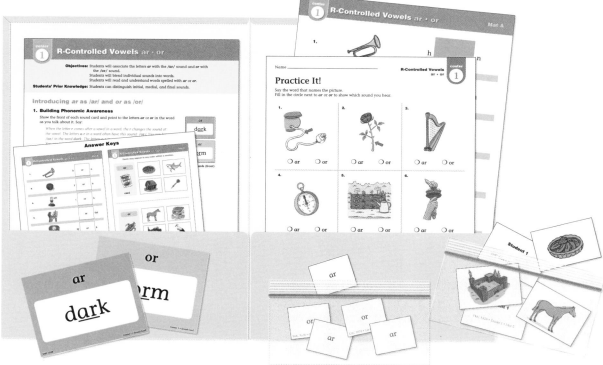

Phonics Intervention Centers
Variant Consonant and Vowel Sounds

EMC 3528 • © Evan-Moor Corp.

Phonics Intervention Centers
Variant Consonant and Vowel Sounds

Group: _____

Date: _____

Group Progress Record

Center _____

Name	Comments	Assessment Level

Phonics Intervention Centers
Variant Consonant and Vowel Sounds

Student Progress Record

	Date / Assessment	Date / Assessment	Date / Assessment
❶ R-Controlled Vowels *ar • or*			
Recognizes the letter pairs that stand for /**ar**/ and /**or**/			
Blends individual sounds into words			
Reads and understands words with the /**ar**/ or the /**or**/ sound			
❷ R-Controlled Vowels *er • ir • ur*			
Recognizes the letter pairs that stand for /**ur**/			
Blends individual sounds into words			
Reads and understands words with the /**ur**/ sound			
❸ R-Controlled Vowels Review			
Reads and understands words with *r*-controlled vowel sounds			
❹ Diphthongs for *oi • oy* and *ou • ow*			
Recognizes the letter pairs that stand for /**oi**/ and /**ou**/			
Blends individual sounds into words			
Reads and understands words with the /**oi**/ or the /**ou**/ diphthong			
❺ Two Sounds of *c*			
Recognizes the /**k**/ and /**s**/ sounds of the letter *c*			
Blends individual sounds into words			
Reads and understands words with the /**k**/ and /**s**/ sounds of *c*			
❻ Two Sounds of *g*			
Recognizes the /**g**/ and /**j**/ sounds of the letter *g*			
Blends individual sounds into words			
Reads and understands words with the /**g**/ and /**j**/ sounds of *g*			
❼ Two Sounds of *s*			
Recognizes the /**s**/ and /**z**/ sounds of the letter *s*			
Blends individual sounds into words			
Reads and understands words with the /**s**/ and /**z**/ sounds of *s*			
❽ Consonant Sounds Review *c • g • s*			
Reads and understands words with variant sounds of *c*, *g*, or *s*			

R-Controlled Vowels
ar · or

For the Teacher

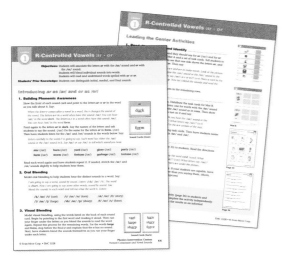

Lesson Plan

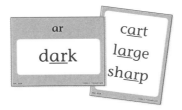
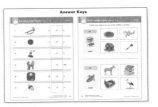

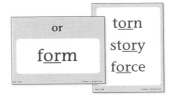

Sound Cards

Answer Keys

For the Student

front (Mat A)

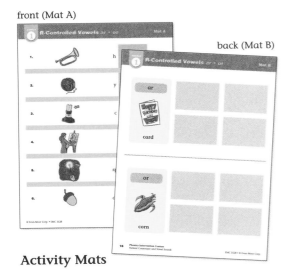

back (Mat B)

Activity Mats

Task Cards

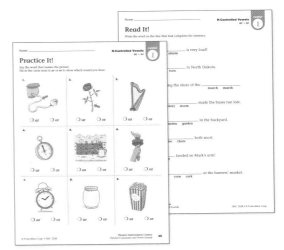

Practice and Assessment Activities

Phonics Intervention Centers
Variant Consonant and Vowel Sounds

EMC 3528 • © Evan-Moor Corp.

R-Controlled Vowels ar • or

Objectives: Students will associate the letters **ar** with the **/ar/** sound and **or** with the **/or/** sound.
Students will blend individual sounds into words.
Students will read and understand words spelled with **ar** or **or**.

Students' Prior Knowledge: Students can distinguish initial, medial, and final sounds.

Introducing *ar* as /ar/ and *or* as /or/

1. Building Phonemic Awareness

Show the front of each sound card and point to the letters **ar** or **or** in the word as you talk about it. Say:

*When the letter **r** comes after a vowel in a word, the **r** changes the sound of the vowel. The letters **a-r** in a word often have this sound: /ar/. You can hear /ar/ in the word **dark**. The letters **o-r** in a word often have this sound: /or/. You can hear /or/ in the word **form**.*

Point again to the letters **ar** in **dark**. Say the names of the letters and ask students to say the sound. (/ar/) Do the same for the letters **or** in **form**. (/or/) Then have students listen for the **/ar/** and **/or/** sounds in the words below. Say:

Listen carefully to the words I'm going to say. Each word has either the /ar/ sound or the /or/ sound in it. Say /ar/ or say /or/ to tell which sound you hear.

Sound Cards (front)

star (/ar/)	born (/or/)	yard (/ar/)	glory (/or/)	party (/ar/)
farm (/ar/)	storm (/or/)	fortune (/or/)	garbage (/ar/)	tortoise (/or/)

Read each word again and have students repeat it. If needed, stretch the **/ar/** and **/or/** sounds slightly to help students hear them.

2. Oral Blending

Model oral blending to help students hear the distinct sounds in a word. Say:

*I am going to say a word, sound by sound. Listen: /ch/ /ar/ /t/. The word is **chart**. Now I am going to say some other words, sound by sound. You blend the sounds in each word and tell me what the word is. Listen:*

/k/ /ar/ /t/ (cart)	/t/ /or/ /n/ (torn)	/st/ /or/ /ē/ (story)
/l/ /ar/ /j/ (large)	/sh/ /ar/ /p/ (sharp)	/f/ /or/ /s/ (force)

3. Visual Blending

Model visual blending, using the words listed on the back of each sound card. Begin by pointing to the first word and reading it aloud. Then run your finger under the letters as you blend the sounds to read the word again. Repeat this process for the remaining words. For the words **large** and **force**, stop before the final **e** and explain that the **e** has no sound. Next, have students blend the sounds themselves as you run your finger under each letter.

Sound Cards (back)

R-Controlled Vowels ar • or (continued)

Leading the Center Activities

1. Read, Discriminate, and Identify

Ask students to tell you the sound they should say for **ar** (/ar/) and for **or** (/or/). Then give each student Mat A and a set of task cards. Tell students to look at both sides of the cards to see that one side shows the letters **ar**, and the other side shows the letters **or**. Then say:

*We are going to use the letters **a-r** and **o-r** to make words. Look at the picture in row 1. It is a horn. Do you hear the /ar/ sound or the /or/ sound in the word **horn**? (/or/) Which letters say /or/: **a-r** or **o-r**? (o-r) Place a card in the box with the letters **o-r** facing up. Now let's blend the sounds and read the word: /h/ /or/ /n/ **horn**.*

Repeat this process with the pictures in the remaining rows.

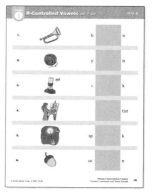

Mat A

2. Read and Understand

Have students turn over their mats. Distribute the task cards for Mat B. Explain that this mat has two sections: one for words with the /ar/ sound as in **card** and one for words with the /or/ sound as in **corn**. Then show the task card that has a picture of a tart on it and say:

*The picture on this card is a tart. Do you hear the /ar/ sound or the /or/ sound in the word **tart**? (/ar/) What letters say /ar/? (a-r) That's right; so we'll place this card in the **a-r** section of the mat.*

Repeat this process with the remaining task cards. Then have students name the pictures on the cards and listen for /ar/ and /or/.

Mat B

3. Practice the Skill

Distribute the Practice It! activity (page 35) to students. Read the directions aloud. Then say:

*Look at the first picture. It is a cord. Say the word **cord**. (cord) What sound do you hear in **cord**: /ar/ or /or/? (/or/) What letters say /or/? (o-r) Now fill in the circle next to the letters **o-r** under the picture.*

Repeat this process to complete the page. If your students are capable, have them say the names of the pictures rather than you saying them. (thorn, harp, north, garden, torch, alarm, jar, popcorn)

Page 35

Apply and Assess

After the lesson, distribute the Read It! activity (page 36) to students and read the directions aloud. Have students complete the activity independently. Then listen to them read the sentences. Use the results as an informal assessment of students' skill mastery.

Page 36

ar

da**rk**

or

fo**rm**

EMC 3528

Answer Keys

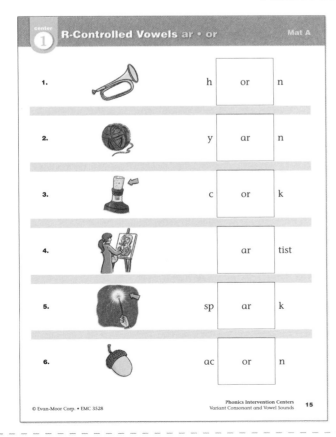

1. h | or | n
2. y | ar | n
3. c | or | k
4. | ar | tist
5. sp | ar | k
6. ac | or | n

© Evan-Moor Corp. • EMC 3528

Phonics Intervention Centers 15
Variant Consonant and Vowel Sounds

Cards may appear in any order within a section.

ar

card

or

corn

16 **Phonics Intervention Centers**
Variant Consonant and Vowel Sounds

EMC 3528 • © Evan-Moor Corp.

torn

st<u>or</u>y

f<u>or</u>ce

Center 1 • Sound Card

c<u>ar</u>t

l<u>ar</u>ge

sh<u>ar</u>p

Center 1 • Sound Card

Answer Keys

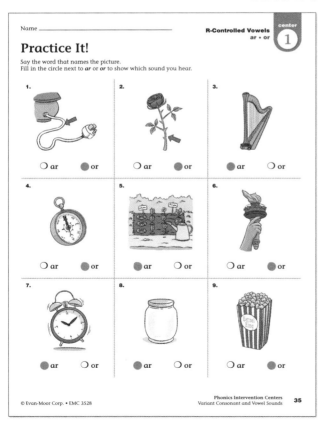

1.  h n

2.   y n

3.  c k

4.  tist

5.  sp k

6.   ac n

ar

card

or

corn

Phonics Intervention Centers
Variant Consonant and Vowel Sounds

EMC 3528 • © Evan-Moor Corp.

1.    h   n

2.   y   n

3.    c   k

4.    tist

5.    sp   k

6.   ac   n

Phonics Intervention Centers
Variant Consonant and Vowel Sounds

EMC 3528 • © Evan-Moor Corp.

1.   h   n

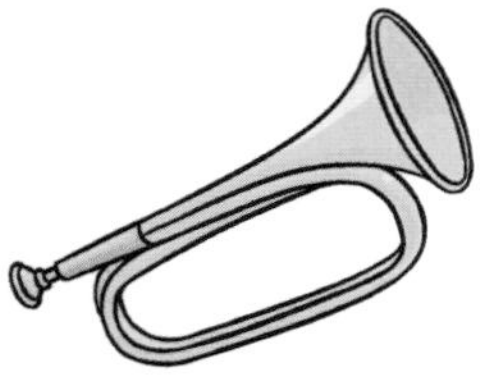

2.   y   n

3.   c   k

4.   tist

5.   sp   k

6.   ac   n

ar

card

or

corn

Phonics Intervention Centers
Variant Consonant and Vowel Sounds

EMC 3528 • © Evan-Moor Corp.

1.   h   n

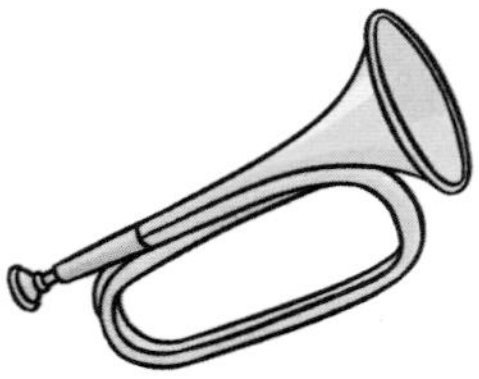

2.   y   n

3.   c   k

4.   tist

5.   sp   k

6.   ac   n

ar

card

or

corn

Phonics Intervention Centers
Variant Consonant and Vowel Sounds

EMC 3528 • © Evan-Moor Corp.

1.  h   n

2. y   n

3.  c   k

4.  tist

5.  sp   k

6. ac   n

ar

card

or

corn

Phonics Intervention Centers
Variant Consonant and Vowel Sounds

EMC 3528 • © Evan-Moor Corp.

1.  h   n

2. y   n

3.  c   k

4.    tist

5.  sp   k

6. ac   n

ar

card

or

corn

Phonics Intervention Centers
Variant Consonant and Vowel Sounds

Student 6	Student 5	Student 4	Student 3	Student 2	Student 1
ar	ar	ar	ar	ar	ar
ar	ar	ar	ar	ar	ar
ar	ar	ar	ar	ar	ar
ar	ar	ar	ar	ar	ar
ar	ar	ar	ar	ar	ar
ar	ar	ar	ar	ar	ar

or

or

or

or

or

or

or

or

or

or

or

or

or

or

or

or

or

or

or

or

or

or

or

or

EMC 3528 • Center 1 • Mat A

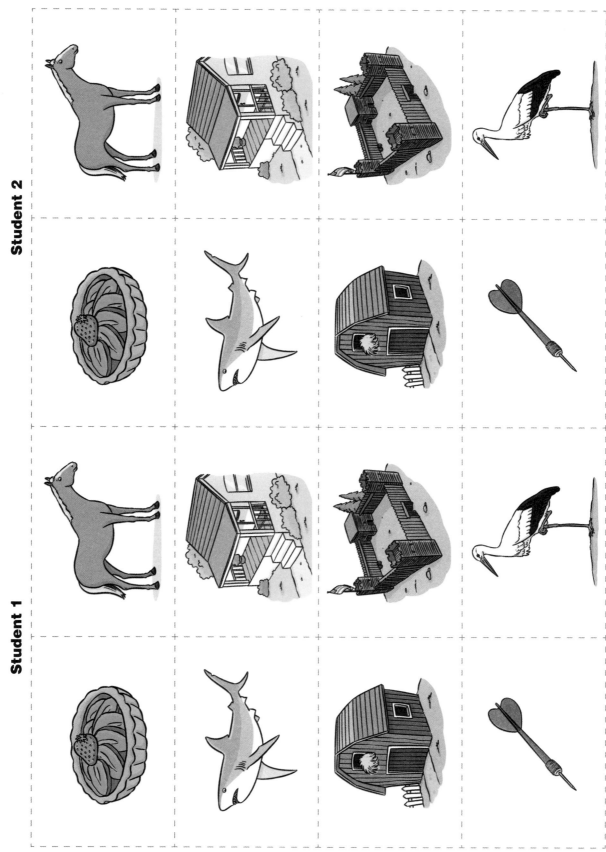

Student 2

Student 1

Student 2

EMC 3528 • Center 1 • Mat B

Student 2

EMC 3528 • Center 1 • Mat B

Student 2

EMC 3528 • Center 1 • Mat B

Student 2

EMC 3528 • Center 1 • Mat B

Student 2

EMC 3528 • Center 1 • Mat B

Student 2

EMC 3528 • Center 1 • Mat B

Student 2

EMC 3528 • Center 1 • Mat B

Student 2

EMC 3528 • Center 1 • Mat B

Student 1

EMC 3528 • Center 1 • Mat B

Student 1

EMC 3528 • Center 1 • Mat B

Student 1

EMC 3528 • Center 1 • Mat B

Student 1

EMC 3528 • Center 1 • Mat B

Student 1

EMC 3528 • Center 1 • Mat B

Student 1

EMC 3528 • Center 1 • Mat B

Student 1

EMC 3528 • Center 1 • Mat B

Phonics Intervention Centers
Variant Consonant and Vowel Sounds

EMC 3528 • © Evan-Moor Corp.

Student 4

Student 3

Student 4

EMC 3528 • Center 1 • Mat B

Student 4

EMC 3528 • Center 1 • Mat B

Student 4

EMC 3528 • Center 1 • Mat B

Student 4

EMC 3528 • Center 1 • Mat B

Student 4

EMC 3528 • Center 1 • Mat B

Student 4

EMC 3528 • Center 1 • Mat B

Student 4

EMC 3528 • Center 1 • Mat B

Student 4

EMC 3528 • Center 1 • Mat B

Student 3

EMC 3528 • Center 1 • Mat B

Student 3

EMC 3528 • Center 1 • Mat B

Student 3

EMC 3528 • Center 1 • Mat B

Student 3

EMC 3528 • Center 1 • Mat B

Student 3

EMC 3528 • Center 1 • Mat B

Student 3

EMC 3528 • Center 1 • Mat B

Student 3

EMC 3528 • Center 1 • Mat B

Student 3

EMC 3528 • Center 1 • Mat B

Phonics Intervention Centers
Variant Consonant and Vowel Sounds

EMC 3528 • © Evan-Moor Corp.

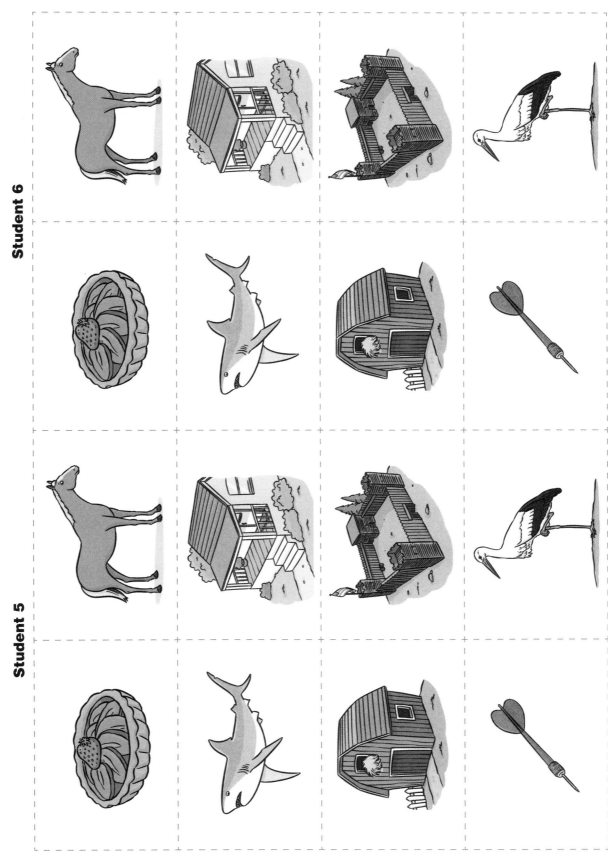

Student 6

Student 5

Student 6

EMC 3528 • Center 1 • Mat B

Student 6

EMC 3528 • Center 1 • Mat B

Student 6

EMC 3528 • Center 1 • Mat B

Student 6

EMC 3528 • Center 1 • Mat B

Student 6

EMC 3528 • Center 1 • Mat B

Student 6

EMC 3528 • Center 1 • Mat B

Student 6

EMC 3528 • Center 1 • Mat B

Student 5

EMC 3528 • Center 1 • Mat B

Student 5

EMC 3528 • Center 1 • Mat B

Student 5

EMC 3528 • Center 1 • Mat B

Student 5

EMC 3528 • Center 1 • Mat B

Student 5

EMC 3528 • Center 1 • Mat B

Student 5

EMC 3528 • Center 1 • Mat B

Student 5

EMC 3528 • Center 1 • Mat B

Practice It!

Say the word that names the picture.
Fill in the circle next to *ar* or *or* to show which sound you hear.

1.

○ ar   ○ or

2.

○ ar   ○ or

3.

○ ar   ○ or

4.

○ ar   ○ or

5.

○ ar   ○ or

6.

○ ar   ○ or

7.

○ ar   ○ or

8.

○ ar   ○ or

9.

○ ar   ○ or

Read It!

Write the word on the line that best completes the sentence.

1. That car _____ is very loud!
harm   alarm

2. Lori was _____ in North Dakota.
born   torn

3. Tall grasses grow along the shore of the _____.
march   marsh

4. A harsh winter _____ made the buses run late.
story   storm

5. Mom planted a _____ in the backyard.
harden   garden

6. A bull and a _____ both snort.
horse   chore

7. A _____ landed on Mark's arm!
shortcut   hornet

8. We can buy fresh _____ at the farmers' market.
corn   cork

center

2

R-Controlled Vowels

er · ir · ur

For the Teacher

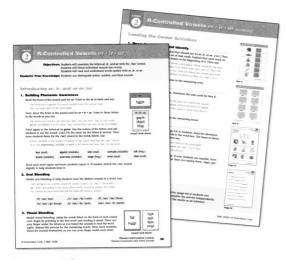

Lesson Plan

ur

turn

er · ir · ur

germ
third
blur

fur

burp

verb
jerk
firm
swirl

Sound Cards

Answer Keys

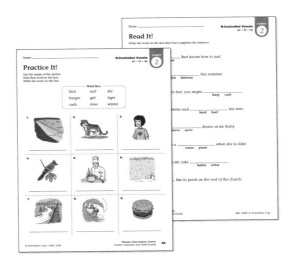

Answer Keys

Answer Keys

For the Student

front (Mat A)

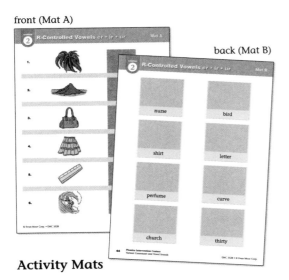

back (Mat B)

Activity Mats

f

p

Task Cards

Practice It!

Read It!

Practice and Assessment Activities

R-Controlled Vowels er • ir • ur

Objectives: Students will associate the letters *er*, *ir*, and **ur** with the /ur/ sound.
Students will blend individual sounds into words.
Students will read and understand words spelled with *er*, *ir*, or **ur**.

Students' Prior Knowledge: Students can distinguish initial, medial, and final sounds.

Introducing *er*, *ir*, and *ur* as /ur/

1. Building Phonemic Awareness

Show the front of the sound card for **ur**. Point to the **ur** in **turn** and say:

> *The letters **u-r** together in a word usually have this sound: /ur/.*
> *You can hear /ur/ in the word **turn**.*

Next, show the front of the sound card for **er • ir • ur**. Point to those letters in the words as you say:

> *The letters **e-r** and **i-r** can also say /ur/. You can hear /ur/ in the words*
> ***germ** and **third**. It is the same /ur/ sound that you hear in the word **blur**.*

Point again to the letters **er** in **germ**. Say the names of the letters and ask students to say the sound. (/ur/) Do the same for the letters **ir** and **ur**. Then have students listen for the /ur/ sound in the words below. Say:

> *Listen carefully to the words I'm going to say. Each word has the /ur/ sound*
> *in it. Say **beginning**, **middle**, or **end** to tell where you hear /ur/ in the word.*

her (end)	**squirt** (middle)	**stir** (end)	**certain** (middle)	**irk** (beg.)
burst (middle)	**nervous** (middle)	**urge** (beg.)	**ever** (end)	**slur** (end)

Read each word again and have students repeat it. If needed, stretch the /ur/ sound slightly to help students hear it.

Sound Cards (front)

ur
turn

er • ir • ur
germ
third
blur

2. Oral Blending

Model oral blending to help students hear the distinct sounds in a word. Say:

> *I am going to say a word, sound by sound. Listen: /s/ /ur/. The word is*
> ***sir**. Now I am going to say some other words, sound by sound. You blend*
> *the sounds in each word and tell me what the word is. Listen:*

/f/ /ur/ (fur)	/v/ /ur/ /b/ (verb)	/f/ /ur/ /m/ (firm)
/b/ /ur/ /p/ (burp)	/j/ /ur/ /k/ (jerk)	/sw/ /ur/ /l/ (swirl)

3. Visual Blending

Model visual blending, using the words listed on the back of each sound card. Begin by pointing to the first word and reading it aloud. Then run your finger under the letters as you blend the sounds to read the word again. Repeat this process for the remaining words. Next, have students blend the sounds themselves as you run your finger under each letter.

fur
burp

verb
jerk
firm
swirl

Sound Cards (back)

Leading the Center Activities

1. Read, Discriminate, and Identify

Ask students to tell you the sound they should say for *er*, *ir*, or *ur*. (/ur/) Then give each student Mat A and a set of task cards. Explain that each word on the mat is missing one or more letters at the beginning of it. Then say:

Look at the picture in row 1. It shows a fern plant. What sound do you hear at the beginning of the word **fern**? *(/f/) What letter says /f/? (f) Place the card with the letter* **f** *on it in the box. Now let's blend the sounds and read the word: /f/ /ur/ /n/ fern. Which two letters in* **fern** *say /ur/? (e-r)*

Repeat this process with the pictures in the remaining rows.

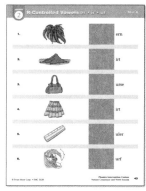

Mat A

2. Read and Understand

Have students turn over their mats. Distribute the task cards for Mat B. Then say:

Look at the word in the first box on the mat. Let's blend the sounds to read the word: /n/ /ur/ /s/ nurse. Which two letters in **nurse** *say /ur/? (u-r) Now find the card that shows a nurse and place it above the word.*

Repeat this process with the words in the remaining boxes.

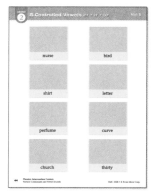

Mat B

3. Practice the Skill

Distribute the Practice It! activity (page 63) to students. Read the directions aloud and have students read the words in the word box. Tell them to blend the sounds as they read each word. Then say:

Look at the first picture. It shows a curb. Point to the word **curb** *in the word box. Which two letters in* **curb** *say /ur/? (u-r) Now write the word* **curb** *on the line under the picture.*

Repeat this process to complete the page. If your students are capable, have them say the names of the pictures rather than you saying them. (tiger, girl, bird, stir, winter, river, surf, burger)

Page 63

Apply and Assess

After the lesson, distribute the Read It! activity (page 64) to students and read the directions aloud. Have students complete the activity independently. Then listen to them read the sentences. Use the results as an informal assessment of students' skill mastery.

Page 64

er • ir • ur

ur

turn

g<u>er</u>m
th<u>ir</u>d
bl<u>ur</u>

EMC 3528

EMC 3528

Center 2 • Sound Card

Answer Keys

center 2 | **R-Controlled Vowels er • ir • ur** | **Mat A**

1. f | ern
2. d | irt
3. p | urse
4. sk | irt
5. r | uler
6. s | urf

center 2 | **R-Controlled Vowels er • ir • ur** | **Mat B**

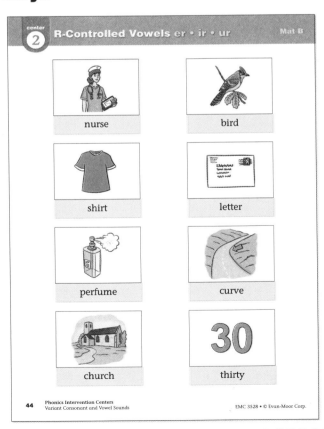

nurse | bird

shirt | letter

perfume | curve

church | 30 thirty

EMC 3528

v<u>er</u>b

j<u>er</u>k

f<u>ir</u>m

sw<u>ir</u>l

f<u>ur</u>

b<u>ur</u>p

Answer Keys

Name _____

R-Controlled Vowels
er • ir • ur

center 2

Practice It!

Say the name of the picture.
Find that word in the box.
Write the word on the line.

Word Box

bird	surf	stir
burger	girl	tiger
curb	river	winter

1. **curb**
2. **tiger**
3. **girl**
4. **bird**
5. **stir**
6. **winter**
7. **river**
8. **surf**
9. **burger**

© Evan-Moor Corp. • EMC 3528

Phonics Intervention Centers
Variant Consonant and Vowel Sounds   **63**

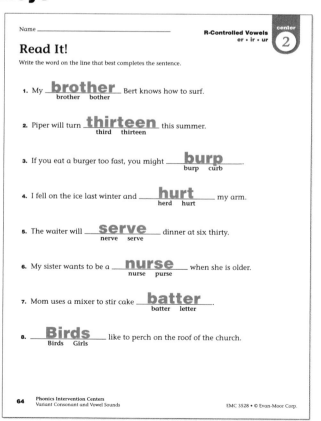

Name _____

R-Controlled Vowels
er • ir • ur

center 2

Read It!

Write the word on the line that best completes the sentence.

1. My **brother** Bert knows how to surf.
   brother   bother

2. Piper will turn **thirteen** this summer.
   third   thirteen

3. If you eat a burger too fast, you might **burp** .
   burp   curb

4. I fell on the ice last winter and **hurt** my arm.
   herd   hurt

5. The waiter will **serve** dinner at six thirty.
   nerve   serve

6. My sister wants to be a **nurse** when she is older.
   nurse   purse

7. Mom uses a mixer to stir cake **batter** .
   batter   letter

8. **Birds** like to perch on the roof of the church.
   Birds   Girls

64 Phonics Intervention Centers
Variant Consonant and Vowel Sounds

EMC 3528 • © Evan-Moor Corp.

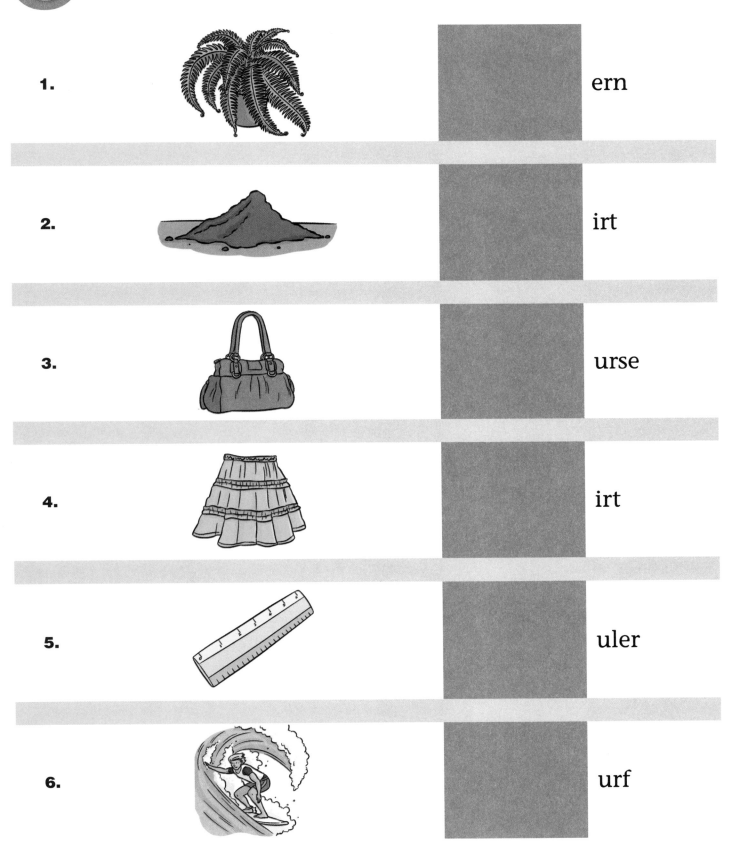

1. ern

2. irt

3. urse

4. irt

5. uler

6. urf

Phonics Intervention Centers
Variant Consonant and Vowel Sounds

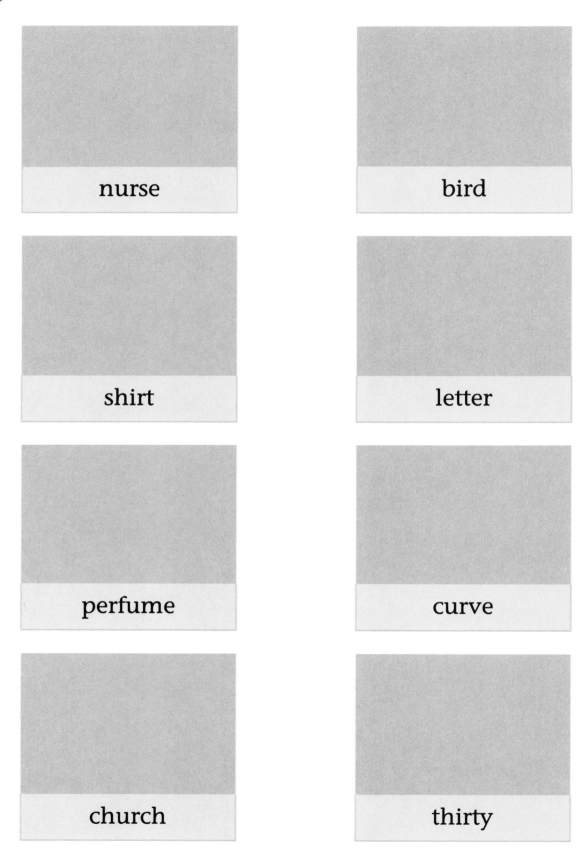

nurse

bird

shirt

letter

perfume

curve

church

thirty

Phonics Intervention Centers
Variant Consonant and Vowel Sounds

EMC 3528 • © Evan-Moor Corp.

1. ern

2. irt

3. urse

4. irt

5. uler

6. urf

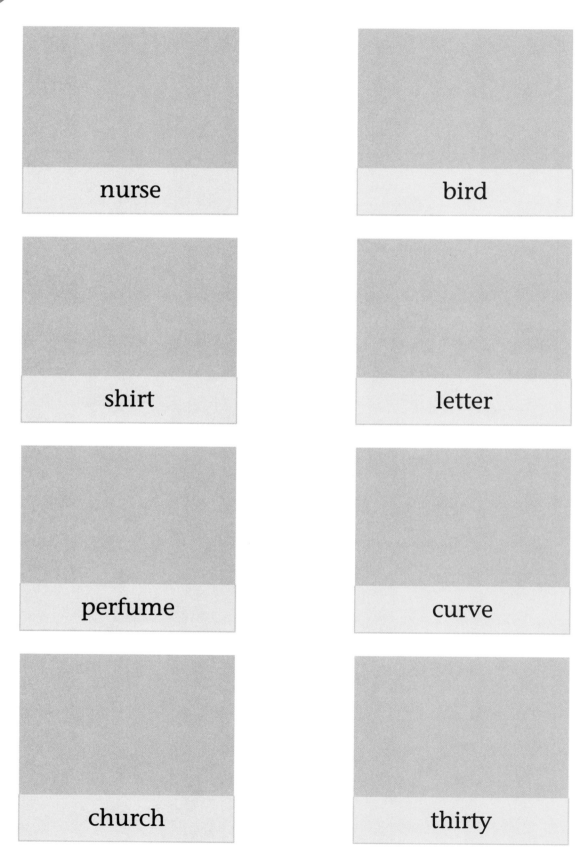

nurse

bird

shirt

letter

perfume

curve

church

thirty

1.  ern

2.  irt

3.  urse

4.  irt

5.  uler

6.  urf

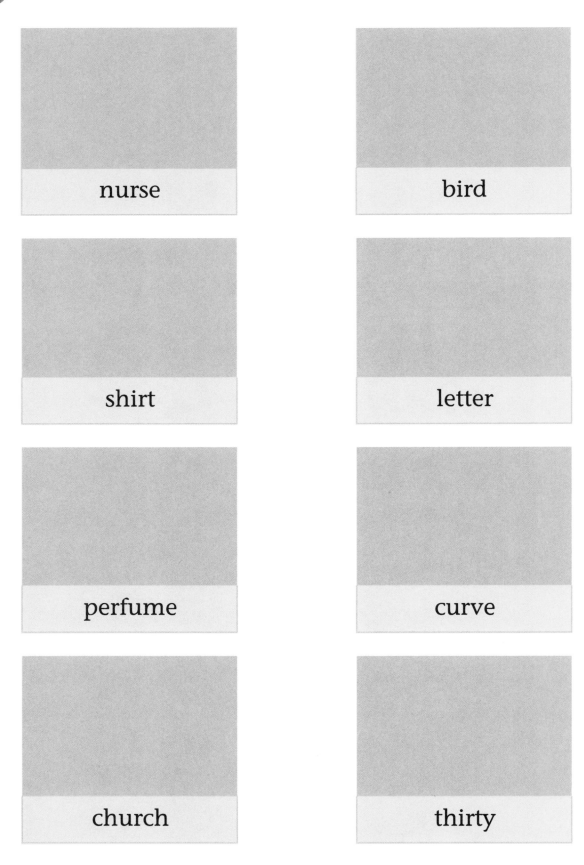

nurse

bird

shirt

letter

perfume

curve

church

thirty

Phonics Intervention Centers
Variant Consonant and Vowel Sounds

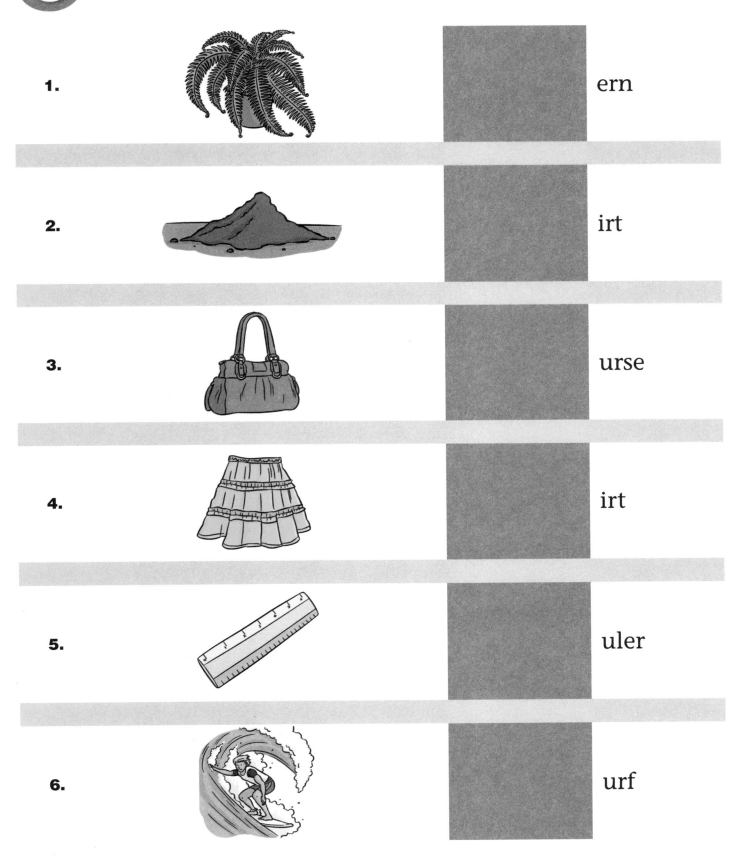

1. ern

2. irt

3. urse

4. irt

5. uler

6. urf

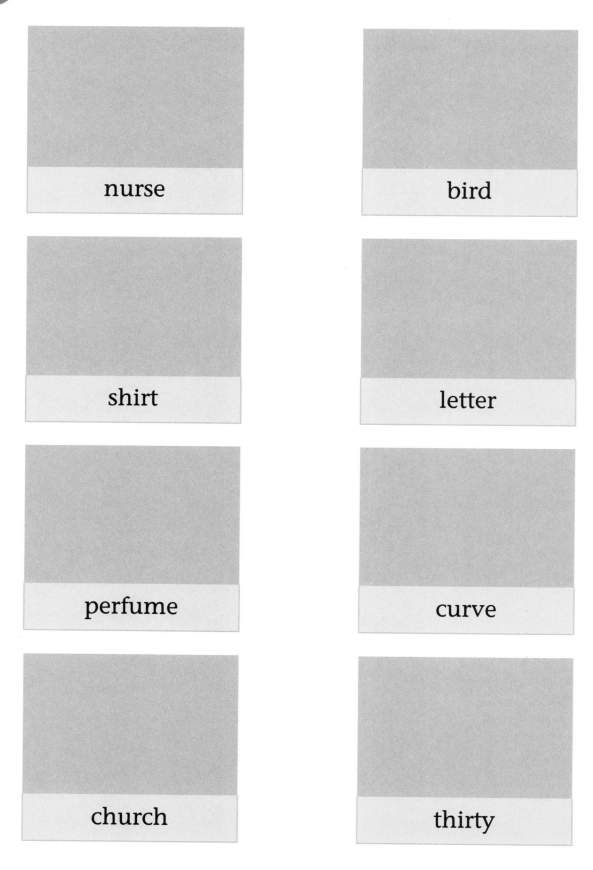

nurse

bird

shirt

letter

perfume

curve

church

thirty

Phonics Intervention Centers
Variant Consonant and Vowel Sounds

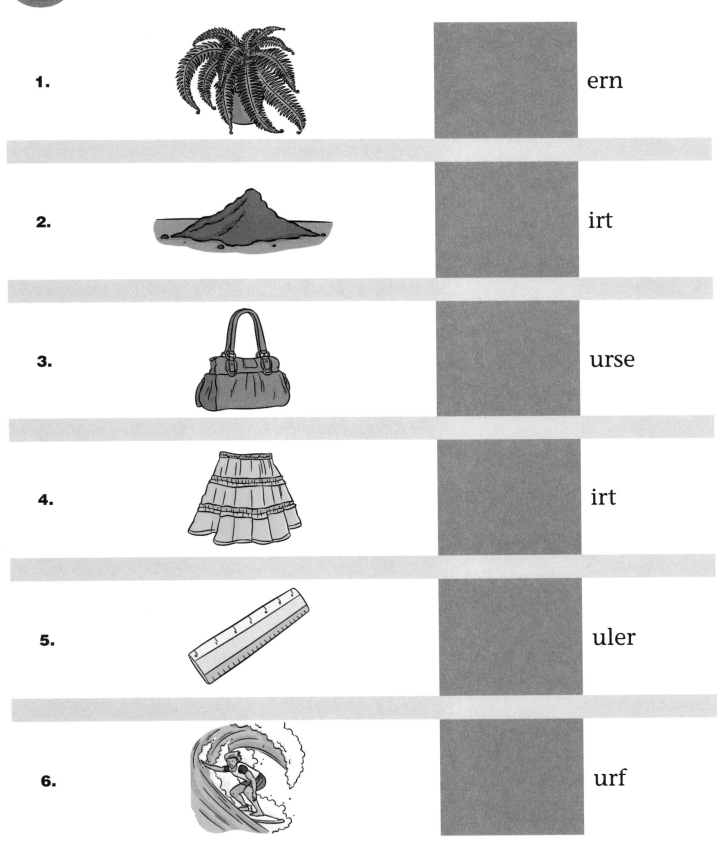

1. ern

2. irt

3. urse

4. irt

5. uler

6. urf

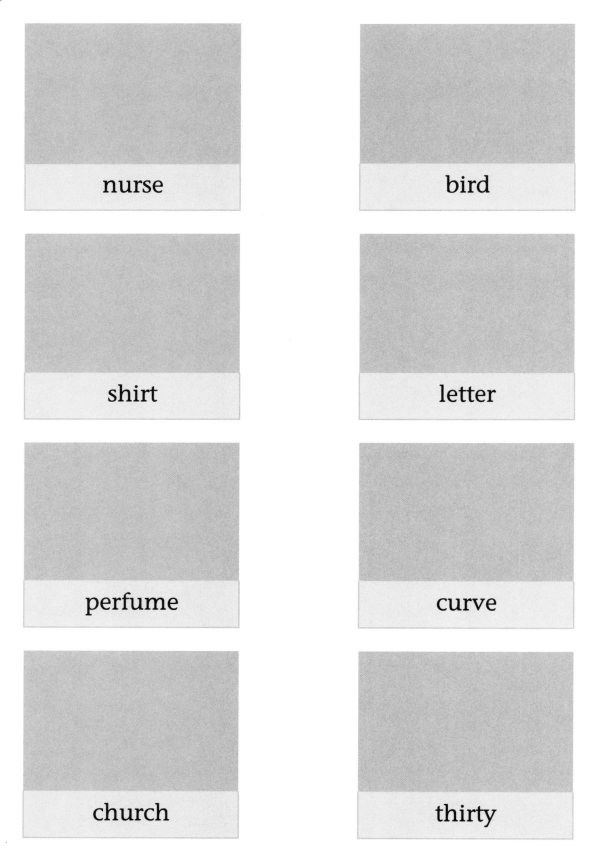

nurse

bird

shirt

letter

perfume

curve

church

thirty

1. ern

2. irt

3. urse

4. irt

5. uler

6. urf

Phonics Intervention Centers
Variant Consonant and Vowel Sounds

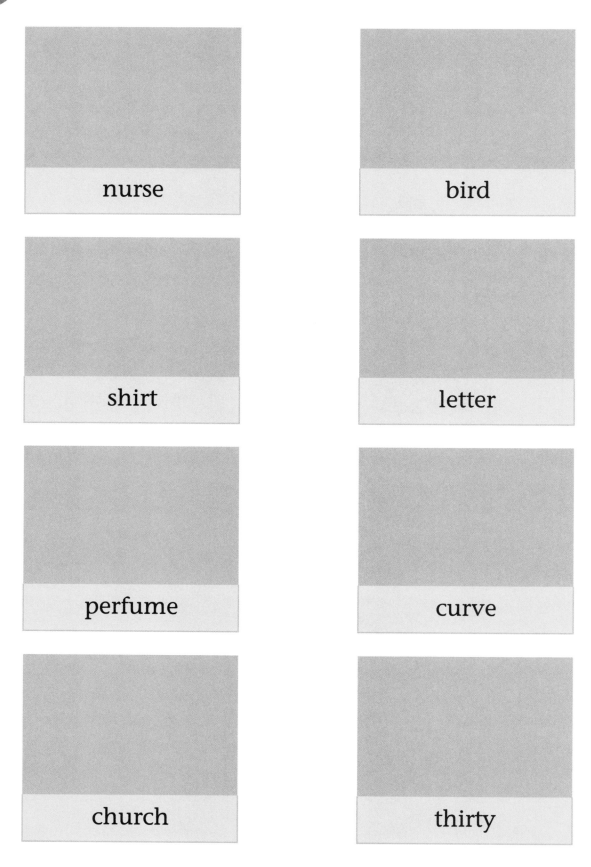

nurse

bird

shirt

letter

perfume

curve

church

thirty

Phonics Intervention Centers
Variant Consonant and Vowel Sounds

EMC 3528 • © Evan-Moor Corp.

	Student 6	Student 5	Student 4	Student 3	Student 2	Student 1
	f	f	f	f	f	f
	d	d	d	d	d	d
	p	p	p	p	p	p
	sk	sk	sk	sk	sk	sk
	r	r	r	r	r	r
	s	s	s	s	s	s

Student 6
EMC 3528
Center 2 • Mat A

Student 6
EMC 3528
Center 2 • Mat A

Student 6
EMC 3528
Center 2 • Mat A

Student 6
EMC 3528
Center 2 • Mat A

Student 6
EMC 3528
Center 2 • Mat A

Student 6
EMC 3528
Center 2 • Mat A

Student 5
EMC 3528
Center 2 • Mat A

Student 5
EMC 3528
Center 2 • Mat A

Student 5
EMC 3528
Center 2 • Mat A

Student 5
EMC 3528
Center 2 • Mat A

Student 5
EMC 3528
Center 2 • Mat A

Student 5
EMC 3528
Center 2 • Mat A

Student 4
EMC 3528
Center 2 • Mat A

Student 4
EMC 3528
Center 2 • Mat A

Student 4
EMC 3528
Center 2 • Mat A

Student 4
EMC 3528
Center 2 • Mat A

Student 4
EMC 3528
Center 2 • Mat A

Student 4
EMC 3528
Center 2 • Mat A

Student 3
EMC 3528
Center 2 • Mat A

Student 3
EMC 3528
Center 2 • Mat A

Student 3
EMC 3528
Center 2 • Mat A

Student 3
EMC 3528
Center 2 • Mat A

Student 3
EMC 3528
Center 2 • Mat A

Student 3
EMC 3528
Center 2 • Mat A

Student 2
EMC 3528
Center 2 • Mat A

Student 2
EMC 3528
Center 2 • Mat A

Student 2
EMC 3528
Center 2 • Mat A

Student 2
EMC 3528
Center 2 • Mat A

Student 2
EMC 3528
Center 2 • Mat A

Student 2
EMC 3528
Center 2 • Mat A

Student 1
EMC 3528
Center 2 • Mat A

Student 1
EMC 3528
Center 2 • Mat A

Student 1
EMC 3528
Center 2 • Mat A

Student 1
EMC 3528
Center 2 • Mat A

Student 1
EMC 3528
Center 2 • Mat A

Student 1
EMC 3528
Center 2 • Mat A

Phonics Intervention Centers
Variant Consonant and Vowel Sounds

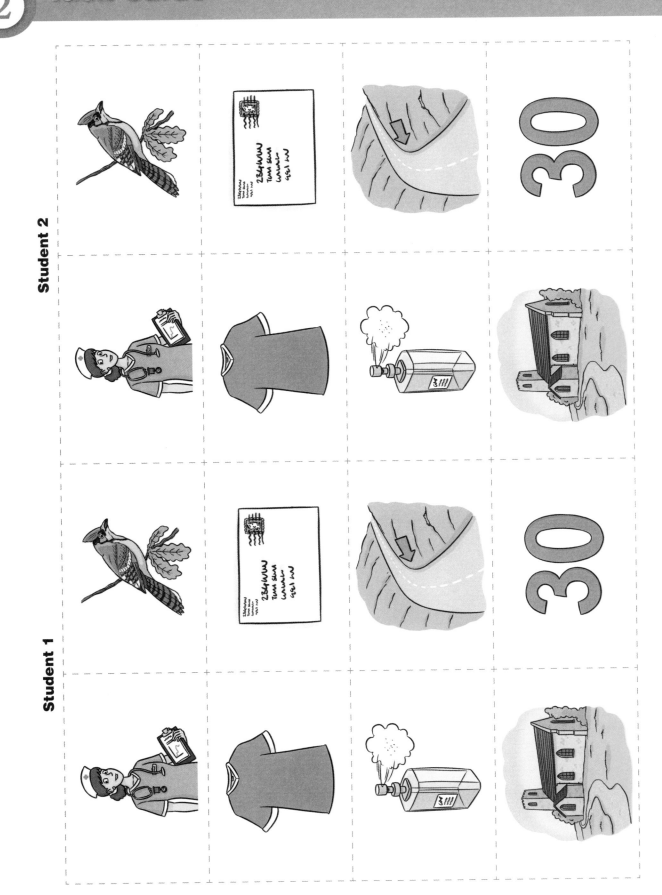

Student 2

Student 1

Student 2

EMC 3528 • Center 2 • Mat B

Student 2

EMC 3528 • Center 2 • Mat B

Student 2

EMC 3528 • Center 2 • Mat B

Student 2

EMC 3528 • Center 2 • Mat B

Student 2

EMC 3528 • Center 2 • Mat B

Student 2

EMC 3528 • Center 2 • Mat B

Student 2

EMC 3528 • Center 2 • Mat B

Student 2

EMC 3528 • Center 2 • Mat B

Student 1

EMC 3528 • Center 2 • Mat B

Student 1

EMC 3528 • Center 2 • Mat B

Student 1

EMC 3528 • Center 2 • Mat B

Student 1

EMC 3528 • Center 2 • Mat B

Student 1

EMC 3528 • Center 2 • Mat B

Student 1

EMC 3528 • Center 2 • Mat B

Student 1

EMC 3528 • Center 2 • Mat B

Student 1

EMC 3528 • Center 2 • Mat B

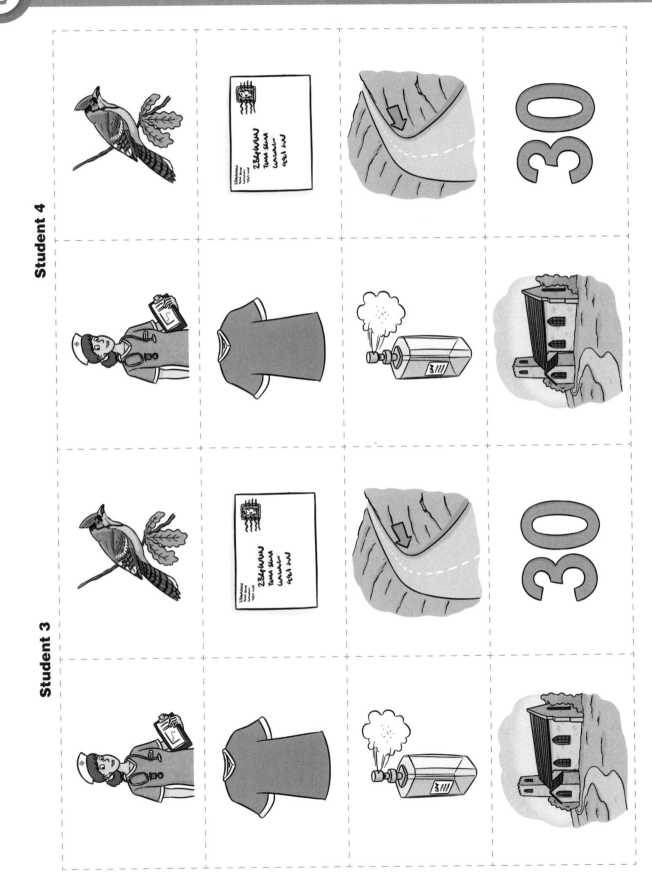

Student 4

Student 3

Student 4

EMC 3528 • Center 2 • Mat B

Student 4

EMC 3528 • Center 2 • Mat B

Student 4

EMC 3528 • Center 2 • Mat B

Student 4

EMC 3528 • Center 2 • Mat B

Student 4

EMC 3528 • Center 2 • Mat B

Student 4

EMC 3528 • Center 2 • Mat B

Student 4

EMC 3528 • Center 2 • Mat B

Student 3

EMC 3528 • Center 2 • Mat B

Student 4

EMC 3528 • Center 2 • Mat B

Student 3

EMC 3528 • Center 2 • Mat B

Student 3

EMC 3528 • Center 2 • Mat B

Student 3

EMC 3528 • Center 2 • Mat B

Student 3

EMC 3528 • Center 2 • Mat B

Student 3

EMC 3528 • Center 2 • Mat B

Student 3

EMC 3528 • Center 2 • Mat B

Student 3

EMC 3528 • Center 2 • Mat B

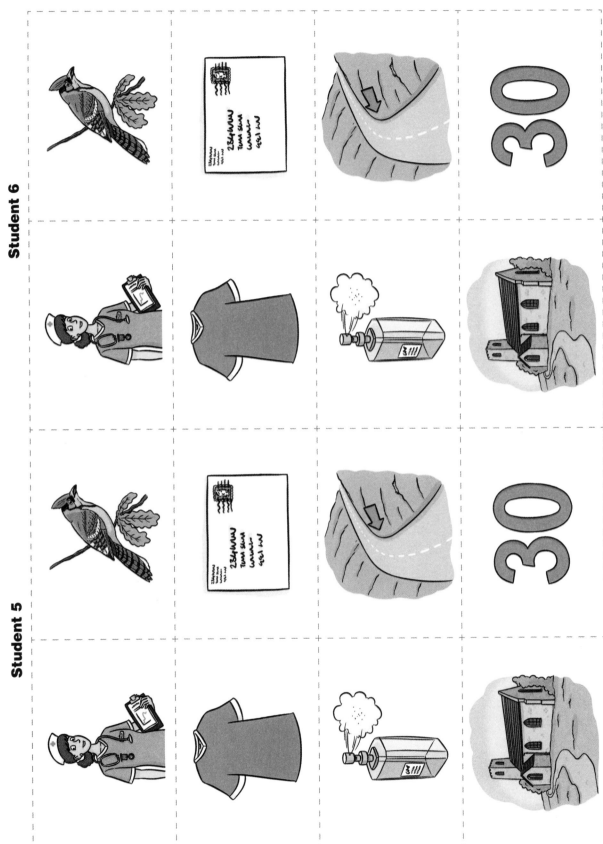

Student 6

Student 5

Student 6

EMC 3528 • Center 2 • Mat B

Student 6

EMC 3528 • Center 2 • Mat B

Student 6

EMC 3528 • Center 2 • Mat B

Student 6

EMC 3528 • Center 2 • Mat B

Student 6

EMC 3528 • Center 2 • Mat B

Student 6

EMC 3528 • Center 2 • Mat B

Student 6

EMC 3528 • Center 2 • Mat B

Student 6

EMC 3528 • Center 2 • Mat B

Student 5

EMC 3528 • Center 2 • Mat B

Student 5

EMC 3528 • Center 2 • Mat B

Student 5

EMC 3528 • Center 2 • Mat B

Student 5

EMC 3528 • Center 2 • Mat B

Student 5

EMC 3528 • Center 2 • Mat B

Student 5

EMC 3528 • Center 2 • Mat B

Student 5

EMC 3528 • Center 2 • Mat B

Student 5

EMC 3528 • Center 2 • Mat B

Name _____

Practice It!

Say the name of the picture.
Find that word in the box.
Write the word on the line.

Word Box

bird	surf	stir
burger	girl	tiger
curb	river	winter

1.

_____

2.

_____

3.

_____

4.

_____

5.

_____

6.

_____

7.

_____

8.

_____

9.

_____

Read It!

Write the word on the line that best completes the sentence.

1. My _____ Bert knows how to surf.
brother   bother

2. Piper will turn _____ this summer.
third   thirteen

3. If you eat a burger too fast, you might _____.
burp   curb

4. I fell on the ice last winter and _____ my arm.
herd   hurt

5. The waiter will _____ dinner at six thirty.
nerve   serve

6. My sister wants to be a _____ when she is older.
nurse   purse

7. Mom uses a mixer to stir cake _____.
batter   letter

8. _____ like to perch on the roof of the church.
Birds   Girls

center

3

R-Controlled Vowels Review

For the Teacher

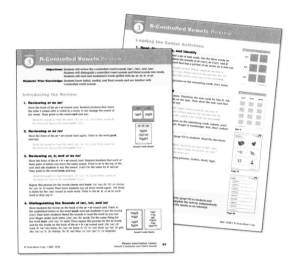

Lesson Plan

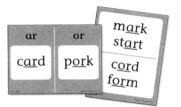

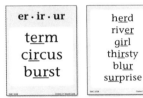

Sound Cards

Answer Keys

For the Student

front (Mat A)

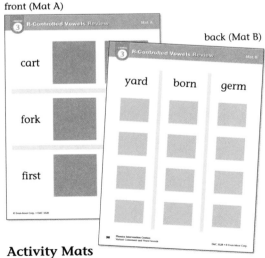

back (Mat B)

Activity Mats

Task Cards

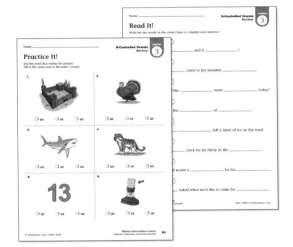

Practice and Assessment Activities

Phonics Intervention Centers
Variant Consonant and Vowel Sounds

EMC 3528 • © Evan-Moor Corp.

R-Controlled Vowels Review

Objectives: Students will review the r-controlled vowel sounds /ar/, /or/, and /ur/.
Students will distinguish r-controlled vowel sounds and blend sounds into words.
Students will read and understand words spelled with *ar, or, er, ir,* or *ur.*

Students' Prior Knowledge: Students know initial, medial, and final sounds and are familiar with *r*-controlled vowel sounds.

Introducing the Review

1. Reviewing *ar* as /ar/

Show the front of the *ar • or* sound card. Remind students that when the letter *r* comes after a vowel in a word, it can change the sound of the vowel. Then point to the word **card** and say:

> *Blend the sounds to read this word.* (/k/ /ar/ /d/ card) *What sound do the letters **a-r** have in the word **card**?* (/ar/)

2. Reviewing *or* as /or/

Show the front of the *ar • or* sound card again. Point to the word **pork** and say:

> *Blend the sounds to read this word.* (/p/ /or/ /k/ pork) *What sound do the letters **o-r** have in the word **pork**?* (/or/)

3. Reviewing *er, ir,* and *ur* as /ur/

Show the front of the *er • ir • ur* sound card. Remind students that each of these pairs of letters can have the same sound. Point to *er* at the top of the card and ask students to say the sound. (/ur/) Do the same for *ir* and *ur*. Then point to the word **term** and say:

> *Blend the sounds to read this word.* (/t/ /ur/ /m/ term) *What sound do the letters **e-r** have in the word **term**?* (/ur/)

Repeat this process for the words **circus** and **burst**. (/s/ /ur/ /k/ /ŭ/ /s/ circus; /b/ /ur/ /s/ /t/ burst) Then have students say all three words again. Tell them to listen for the **/ur/** sound in each word. Point to the *er, ir,* or *ur* in each word as they say it.

4. Distinguishing the Sounds of /ar/, /or/, and /ur/

Show students the words on the back of the *ar • or* sound card. Point to the underlined letters in the word **mark** and ask students to say the sound. (/ar/) Then have students blend the sounds to read the word as you run your finger under each letter. (/m/ /ar/ /k/ mark) Do the same thing for the word **start**. (/st/ /ar/ /t/ start) Then repeat this process for the *or* words and for the words on the back of the *er • ir • ur* sound card. (/k/ /or/ /d/ cord; /f/ /or/ /m/ form; /h/ /ur/ /d/ herd; /r/ /ĭ/ /v/ /ur/ river; /g/ /ur/ /l/ girl; /th/ /ur/ /s/ /t/ /ē/ thirsty; /b/ /l/ /ur/ blur; /s/ /ur/ /pr/ /ī/ /z/ surprise)

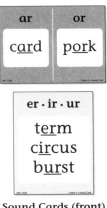

ar	or
c**ar**d	p**or**k

er · ir · ur
t**er**m
c**ir**cus
b**ur**st

Sound Cards (front)

m**ar**k	h**er**d
st**ar**t	r**i**v**er**
	g**ir**l
c**or**d	th**ir**sty
f**or**m	bl**ur**
	s**ur**prise

Sound Cards (back)

Leading the Center Activities

1. Read, Discriminate, and Identify

Give each student Mat A and a set of task cards. Use the three words on the mat to review with students the sounds of *ar* (/ar/), *or* (/or/), and *ir* (/ur/). Then show the task card that has a picture of an acorn on it and say:

What is the picture on this card? (acorn) *Which sound do you hear in* **acorn**: /ar/, /or/, or /ur/? (/or/) *Which word on the mat also has the* /or/ *sound?* (fork) *Now place this card in a box next to the word* **fork**.

Repeat this process with the pictures on the remaining cards. (tart, harp; horn; skirt, bird)

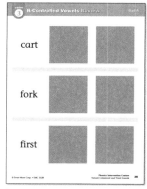

Mat A

2. Read and Understand

Have students turn over their mats. Distribute the task cards for Mat B. Ask students to read the three words on the mat. Then show the task card that has a picture of a dart on it and say:

What is the picture on this card? (dart) *Which sound do you hear in* **dart**: /ar/, /or/, or /ur/? (/ar/) *Which word on the mat also has the* /ar/ *sound?* (yard) *Now place this card in a box under the word* **yard**.

Repeat this process with the pictures on the remaining cards. (alarm, scarf, target; torch, orange, thorn, organ; burger or hamburger, fern, shirt, turkey)

Mat B

3. Practice the Skill

Distribute the Practice It! activity (page 93) to students. Read the directions aloud. Then say:

What is the first picture? (fort) *Which sound do you hear in* **fort**: /ar/, /or/, or /ur/? (/or/) *Which pair of letters below the picture say* /or/? (o-r) *Now fill in the circle next to the letters* **o-r**.

Repeat this process with the remaining pictures. (turkey, shark, tiger, thirteen, cork)

Page 93

Apply and Assess

After the lesson, distribute the Read It! activity (page 94) to students and read the directions aloud. Have students complete the activity independently. Then listen to them read the sentences. Use the results as an informal assessment of students' skill mastery.

Page 94

EMC 3528

or

ar

p<u>or</u>k

c<u>ar</u>d

er · ir · ur

t<u>er</u>m

<u>cir</u>cus

b<u>ur</u>st

EMC 3528

Answer Keys

center 3 — R-Controlled Vowels Review — Mat A

Cards may appear in any order within a section.

cart

fork

first

Phonics Intervention Centers
Variant Consonant and Vowel Sounds **35**

center 3 — R-Controlled Vowels Review — Mat B

Cards may appear in any order within a column.

yard   born   germ

36 **Phonics Intervention Centers**
Variant Consonant and Vowel Sounds

EMC 3528 • © Evan-Moor Corp.

herd
river
girl
thirsty
blur
surprise

Center 3 • Sound Card

mark
start

cord
form

Center 3 • Sound Card

Answer Keys

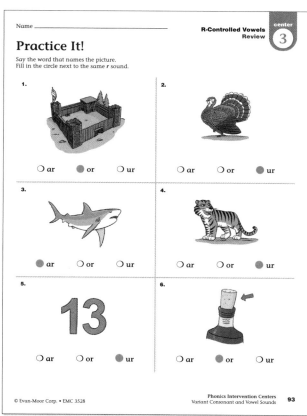

cart

fork

first

yard   born   germ

Phonics Intervention Centers
Variant Consonant and Vowel Sounds

EMC 3528 • © Evan-Moor Corp.

cart

fork

first

yard   born   germ

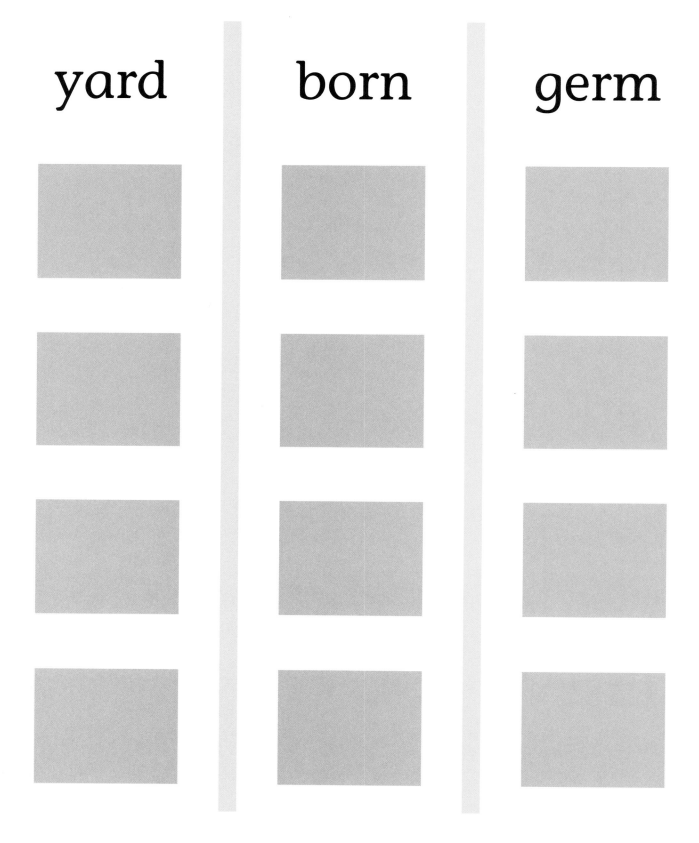

Phonics Intervention Centers
Variant Consonant and Vowel Sounds

EMC 3528 • © Evan-Moor Corp.

cart

fork

first

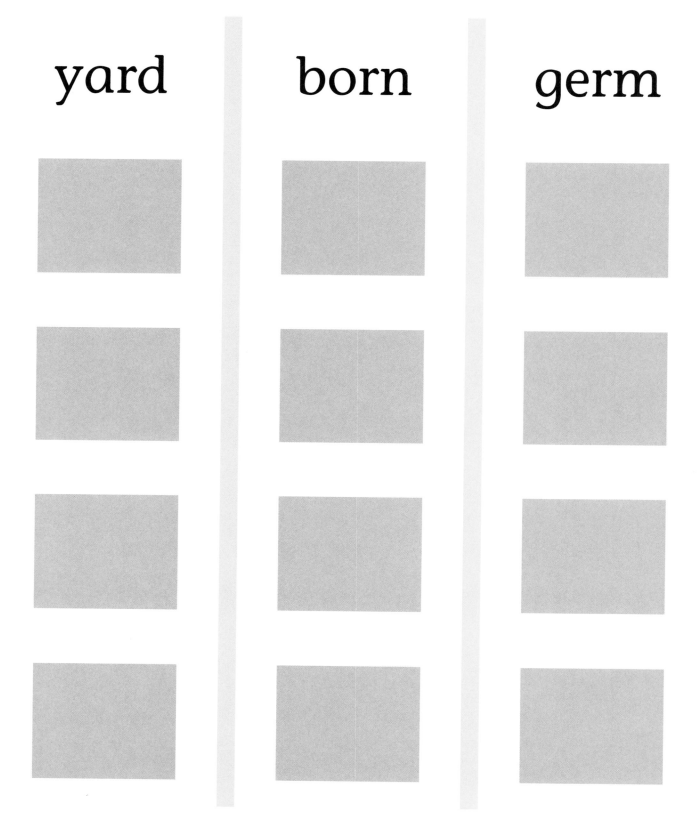

yard

born

germ

Phonics Intervention Centers
Variant Consonant and Vowel Sounds

EMC 3528 • © Evan-Moor Corp.

cart

fork

first

yard | born | germ

Phonics Intervention Centers
Variant Consonant and Vowel Sounds

EMC 3528 • © Evan-Moor Corp.

cart

fork

first

yard born germ

Phonics Intervention Centers
Variant Consonant and Vowel Sounds

EMC 3528 • © Evan-Moor Corp.

cart

fork

first

yard   born   germ

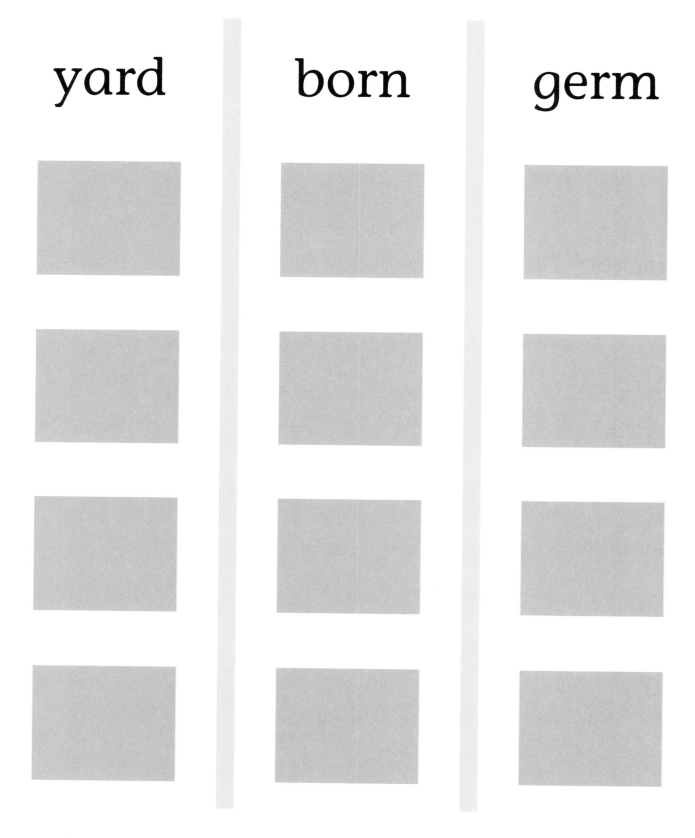

Student 2

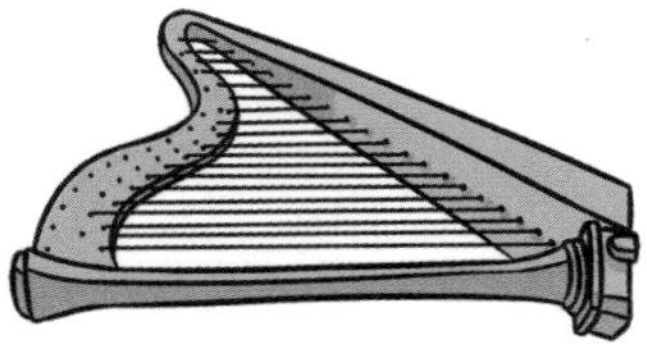

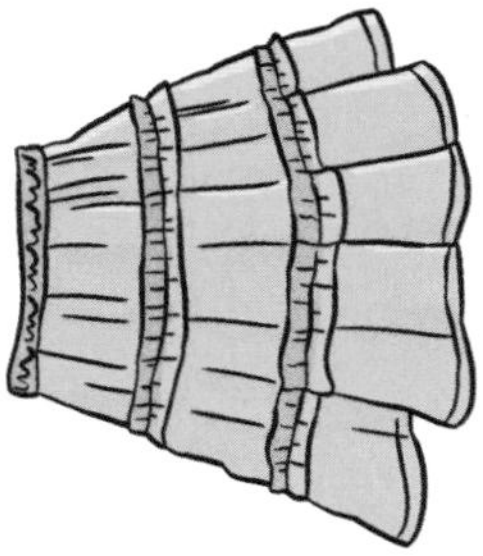

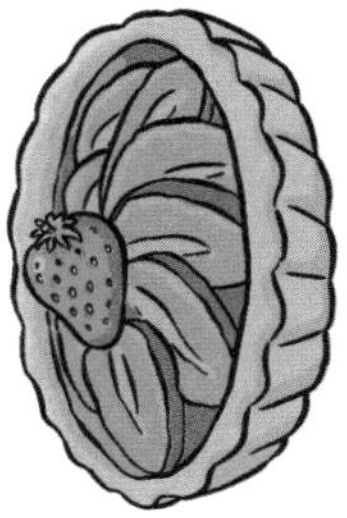

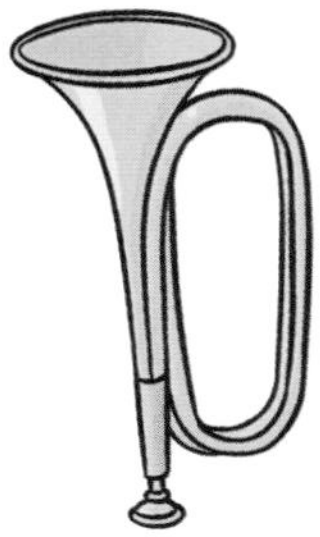

Student 1

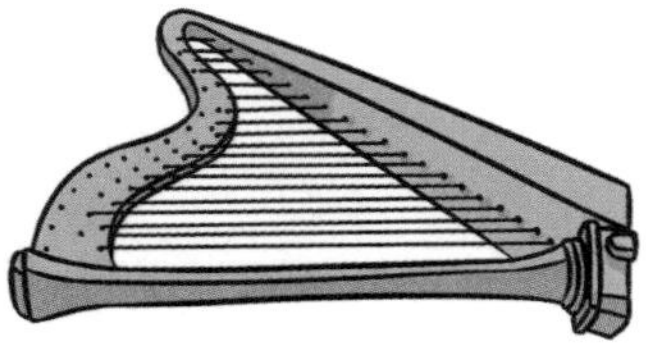

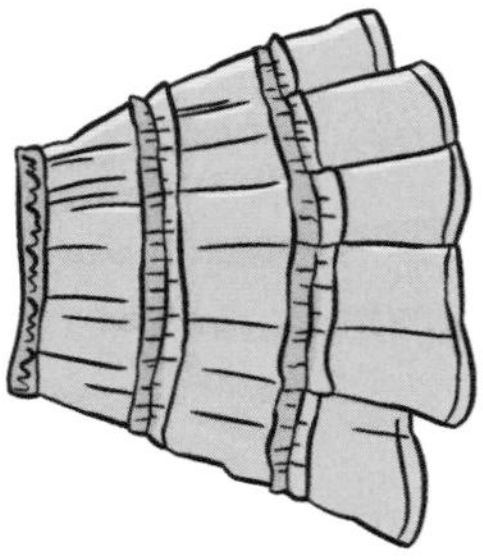

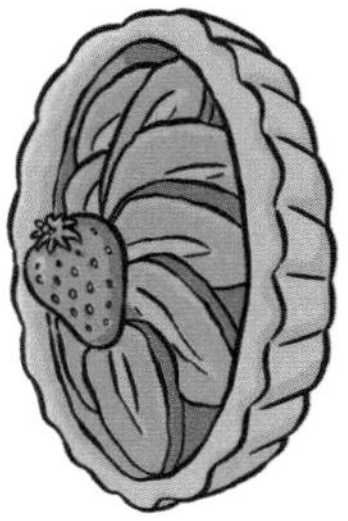

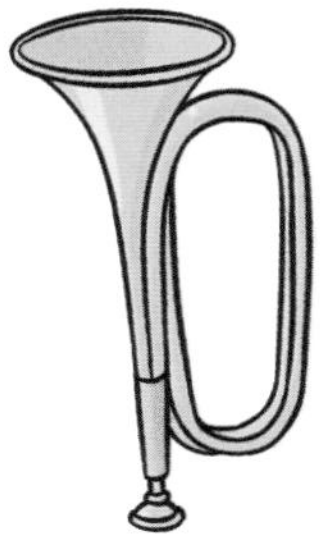

Student 2

EMC 3528 • Center 3 • Mat A

Student 2

EMC 3528 • Center 3 • Mat A

Student 2

EMC 3528 • Center 3 • Mat A

Student 2

EMC 3528 • Center 3 • Mat A

Student 2

EMC 3528 • Center 3 • Mat A

Student 2

EMC 3528 • Center 3 • Mat A

Student 1

EMC 3528 • Center 3 • Mat A

Student 1

EMC 3528 • Center 3 • Mat A

Student 1

EMC 3528 • Center 3 • Mat A

Student 1

EMC 3528 • Center 3 • Mat A

Student 1

EMC 3528 • Center 3 • Mat A

Student 1

EMC 3528 • Center 3 • Mat A

Phonics Intervention Centers
Variant Consonant and Vowel Sounds

EMC 3528 • © Evan-Moor Corp.

Student 4

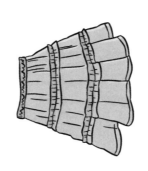

Student 3

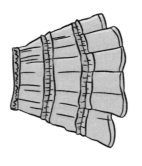

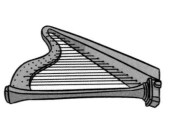

Phonics Intervention Centers
Variant Consonant and Vowel Sounds

Student 4

EMC 3528 • Center 3 • Mat A

Student 4

EMC 3528 • Center 3 • Mat A

Student 4

EMC 3528 • Center 3 • Mat A

Student 4

EMC 3528 • Center 3 • Mat A

Student 4

EMC 3528 • Center 3 • Mat A

Student 3

EMC 3528 • Center 3 • Mat A

Student 3

EMC 3528 • Center 3 • Mat A

Student 3

EMC 3528 • Center 3 • Mat A

Student 3

EMC 3528 • Center 3 • Mat A

Student 3

EMC 3528 • Center 3 • Mat A

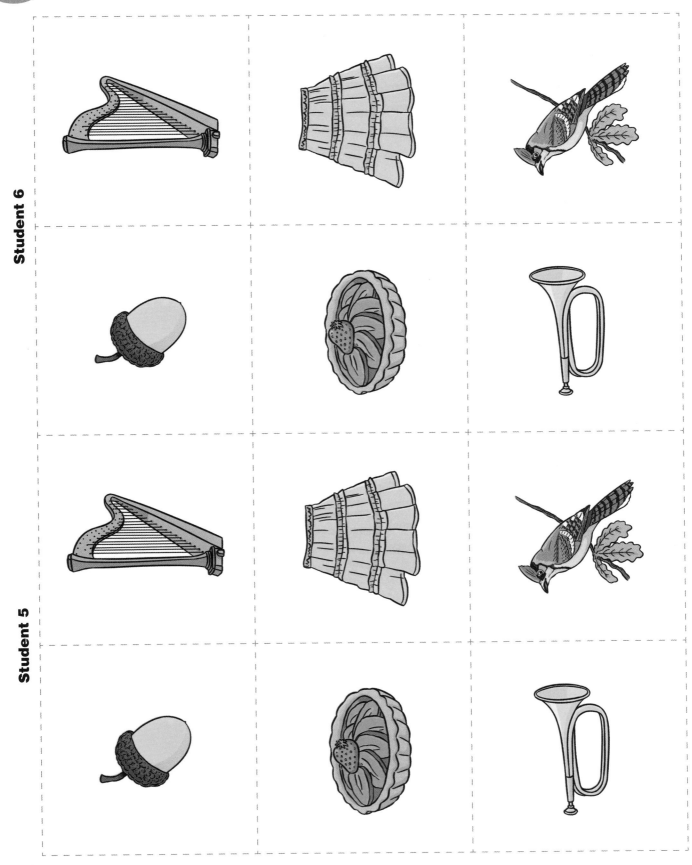

Student 6

Student 5

Student 6

EMC 3528 • Center 3 • Mat A

Student 6

EMC 3528 • Center 3 • Mat A

Student 6

EMC 3528 • Center 3 • Mat A

Student 6

EMC 3528 • Center 3 • Mat A

Student 6

EMC 3528 • Center 3 • Mat A

Student 6

EMC 3528 • Center 3 • Mat A

Student 5

EMC 3528 • Center 3 • Mat A

Student 5

EMC 3528 • Center 3 • Mat A

Student 5

EMC 3528 • Center 3 • Mat A

Student 5

EMC 3528 • Center 3 • Mat A

Student 5

EMC 3528 • Center 3 • Mat A

Student 5

EMC 3528 • Center 3 • Mat A

Phonics Intervention Centers
Variant Consonant and Vowel Sounds

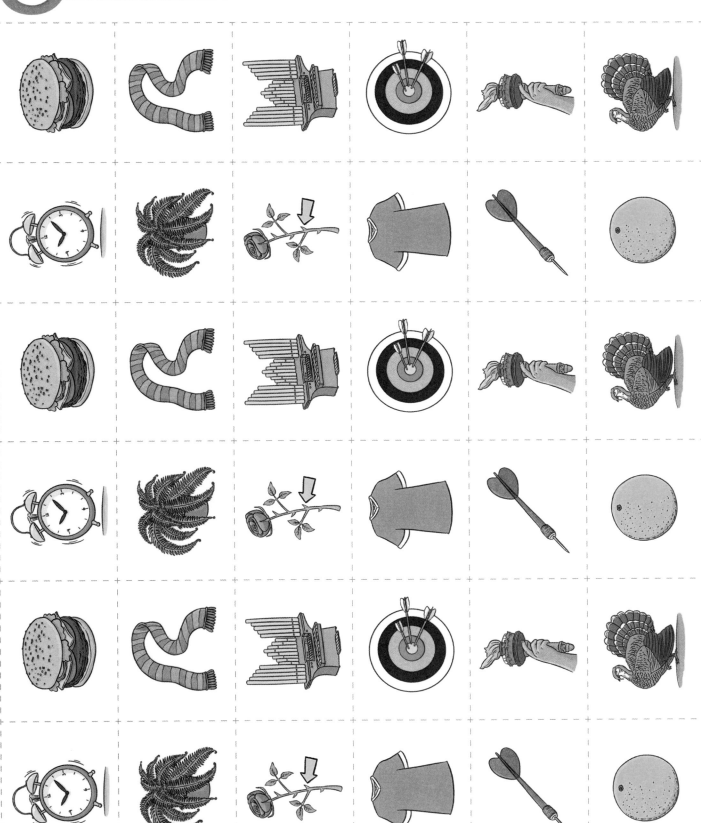

Student 3
EMC 3528
Center 3 • Mat B

Student 3
EMC 3528
Center 3 • Mat B

Student 3
EMC 3528
Center 3 • Mat B

Student 3
EMC 3528
Center 3 • Mat B

Student 3
EMC 3528
Center 3 • Mat B

Student 3
EMC 3528
Center 3 • Mat B

Student 3
EMC 3528
Center 3 • Mat B

Student 3
EMC 3528
Center 3 • Mat B

Student 2
EMC 3528
Center 3 • Mat B

Student 2
EMC 3528
Center 3 • Mat B

Student 2
EMC 3528
Center 3 • Mat B

Student 2
EMC 3528
Center 3 • Mat B

Student 2
EMC 3528
Center 3 • Mat B

Student 2
EMC 3528
Center 3 • Mat B

Student 2
EMC 3528
Center 3 • Mat B

Student 2
EMC 3528
Center 3 • Mat B

Student 1
EMC 3528
Center 3 • Mat B

Student 1
EMC 3528
Center 3 • Mat B

Student 1
EMC 3528
Center 3 • Mat B

Student 1
EMC 3528
Center 3 • Mat B

Student 1
EMC 3528
Center 3 • Mat B

Student 1
EMC 3528
Center 3 • Mat B

Student 1
EMC 3528
Center 3 • Mat B

Student 1
EMC 3528
Center 3 • Mat B

Phonics Intervention Centers
Variant Consonant and Vowel Sounds

EMC 3528 • © Evan-Moor Corp.

Student 6

Student 5

Student 4

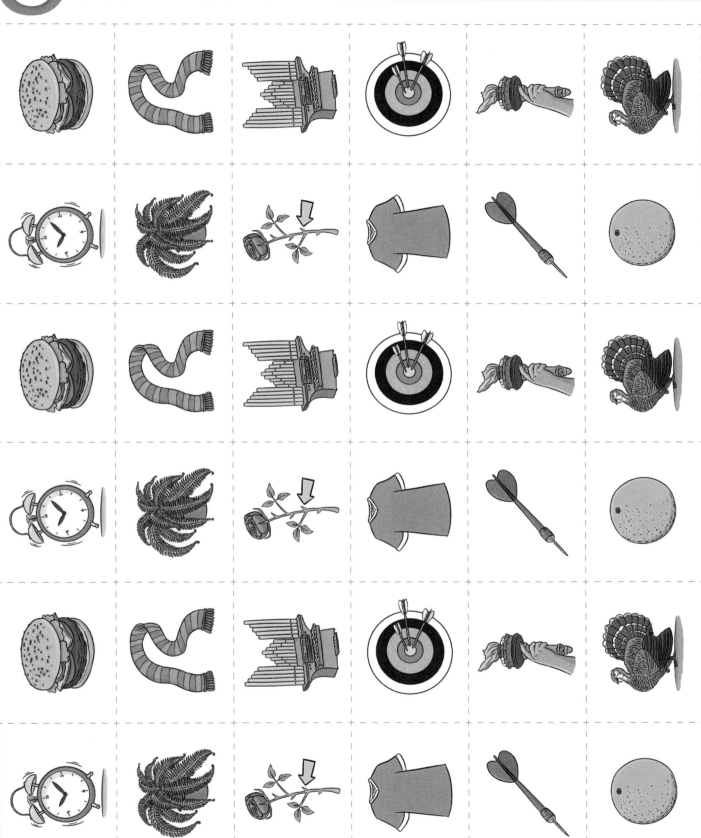

Student 6
EMC 3528
Center 3 • Mat B
EMC 3528
Center 3 • Mat B

Student 6
EMC 3528
Center 3 • Mat B
EMC 3528
Center 3 • Mat B

Student 6
EMC 3528
Center 3 • Mat B
EMC 3528
Center 3 • Mat B

Student 6
EMC 3528
Center 3 • Mat B
EMC 3528
Center 3 • Mat B

Student 6
EMC 3528
Center 3 • Mat B
EMC 3528
Center 3 • Mat B

Student 6
EMC 3528
Center 3 • Mat B
EMC 3528
Center 3 • Mat B

Student 6
EMC 3528
Center 3 • Mat B
EMC 3528
Center 3 • Mat B

Student 6
EMC 3528
Center 3 • Mat B
EMC 3528
Center 3 • Mat B

Student 5
EMC 3528
Center 3 • Mat B
EMC 3528
Center 3 • Mat B

Student 5
EMC 3528
Center 3 • Mat B
EMC 3528
Center 3 • Mat B

Student 5
EMC 3528
Center 3 • Mat B
EMC 3528
Center 3 • Mat B

Student 5
EMC 3528
Center 3 • Mat B
EMC 3528
Center 3 • Mat B

Student 5
EMC 3528
Center 3 • Mat B
EMC 3528
Center 3 • Mat B

Student 5
EMC 3528
Center 3 • Mat B
EMC 3528
Center 3 • Mat B

Student 5
EMC 3528
Center 3 • Mat B
EMC 3528
Center 3 • Mat B

Student 5
EMC 3528
Center 3 • Mat B
EMC 3528
Center 3 • Mat B

Student 4
EMC 3528
Center 3 • Mat B
EMC 3528
Center 3 • Mat B

Student 4
EMC 3528
Center 3 • Mat B
EMC 3528
Center 3 • Mat B

Student 4
EMC 3528
Center 3 • Mat B
EMC 3528
Center 3 • Mat B

Student 4
EMC 3528
Center 3 • Mat B
EMC 3528
Center 3 • Mat B

Student 4
EMC 3528
Center 3 • Mat B
EMC 3528
Center 3 • Mat B

Student 4
EMC 3528
Center 3 • Mat B
EMC 3528
Center 3 • Mat B

Student 4
EMC 3528
Center 3 • Mat B
EMC 3528
Center 3 • Mat B

Student 4
EMC 3528
Center 3 • Mat B
EMC 3528
Center 3 • Mat B

Practice It!

Say the word that names the picture.
Fill in the circle next to the same *r* sound.

1.

○ ar   ○ or   ○ ur

2.

○ ar   ○ or   ○ ur

3.

○ ar   ○ or   ○ ur

4.

○ ar   ○ or   ○ ur

5.

○ ar   ○ or   ○ ur

6.

○ ar   ○ or   ○ ur

Name _____

Read It!

Write the two words on the correct lines to complete each sentence.

1. (finger   hurts)

   I burned my _____, and it _____!

2. (girls   party)

   Thirteen _____ came to my slumber _____.

3. (score   soccer)

   How many goals did the _____ team _____ today?

4. (church   organ)

   My sister Nora plays the _____ at _____.

5. (storm   winter)

   The _____ _____ left a layer of ice on the road.

6. (alarm   morning)

   I set my _____ clock for six thirty in the _____.

7. (birthday   car)

   My older brother Kurt wants a _____ for his _____.

8. (dinner   waiter)

   The _____ asked what we'd like to order for _____.

center

4

Diphthongs for oi · oy and ou · ow

For the Teacher

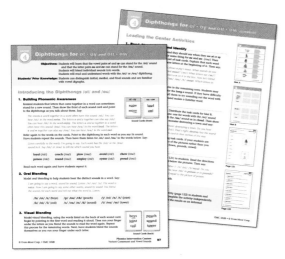

Lesson Plan

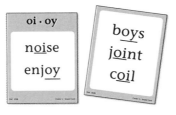

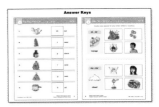

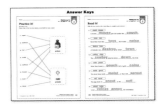

Sound Cards

Answer Keys

For the Student

front (Mat A)

back (Mat B)

Activity Mats

Task Cards

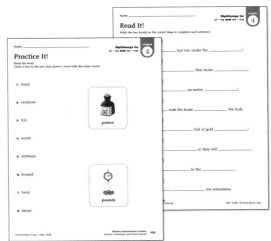

Practice and Assessment Activities

EMC 3528 • © Evan-Moor Corp.

Diphthongs for oi · oy and ou · ow

Objectives: Students will learn that the vowel pairs *oi* and *oy* can stand for the /oi/ sound and that the letter pairs *ou* and *ow* can stand for the /ou/ sound.
Students will blend individual sounds into words.
Students will read and understand words with the /oi/ or /ou/ diphthong.

Students' Prior Knowledge: Students can distinguish initial, medial, and final sounds and are familiar with vowel digraphs.

Introducing the Diphthongs /oi/ and /ou/

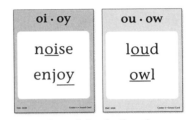

Sound Cards (front)

1. Building Phonemic Awareness

Remind students that letters that come together in a word can sometimes stand for a new sound. Then show the front of each sound card and point to the diphthongs as you talk about them. Say:

*The vowels **o** and **i** together in a word often have this sound: /oi/. You can hear /oi/ in the word **noise**. The letters **o** and **y** together can also say /oi/. You can hear /oi/ in the word **enjoy**. The letters **o** and **u** together in a word often have this sound: /ou/. You can hear /ou/ in the word **loud**. The letters **o** and **w** together can also say /ou/. You can hear /ou/ in the word **owl**.*

Refer again to the words on the cards. Point to the diphthong in each word as you say its sound. Have students repeat the sounds. Then have them listen for /oi/ and /ou/ in the words below. Say:

Listen carefully to the words I'm going to say. Each word has the /oi/ or the /ou/ sound in it. Say /oi/ or /ou/ to tell me which sound you hear.

loyal (/oi/)	**couch** (/ou/)	**plow** (/ou/)	**avoid** (/oi/)	**chow** (/ou/)
poison (/oi/)	**round** (/ou/)	**employ** (/oi/)	**oyster** (/oi/)	**proud** (/ou/)

Read each word again and have students repeat it.

2. Oral Blending

Model oral blending to help students hear the distinct sounds in a word. Say:

*I am going to say a word, sound by sound. Listen: /v/ /oi/ /s/. The word is **voice**. Now I am going to say some other words, sound by sound. You blend the sounds for each word and tell me what the word is. Listen:*

/b/ /oi/ /z/ (boys)	/p/ /ou/ /ch/ (pouch)	/j/ /oi/ /n/ /t/ (joint)
/k/ /oi/ /l/ (coil)	/s/ /ou/ /n/ /d/ (sound)	/t/ /ou/ /ur/ (tower)

3. Visual Blending

Model visual blending, using the words listed on the back of each sound card. Begin by pointing to the first word and reading it aloud. Then run your finger under the letters as you blend the sounds to read the word again. Repeat this process for the remaining words. Next, have students blend the sounds themselves as you run your finger under each letter.

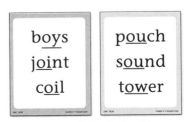

Sound Cards (back)

Leading the Center Activities

1. Read, Discriminate, and Identify ....

Ask students to tell you the sound they should say when they see **oi** or **oy** together in a word. (/oi/) Do the same thing for **ou** and **ow**. (/ou/) Then give each student Mat A and a set of task cards. Explain that each word on the mat is missing one or more letters at the beginning of it. Then say:

*Look at the picture in row 1. It shows a pig's snout. What sounds do you hear at the beginning of the word **snout**? (/sn/) What letters say /sn/?* (s-n) *Place the card with the letters **s-n** on it in the box. Now let's blend the sounds and read the word: /sn/ /ou/ /t/ snout. Which letters in* **snout** *say /ou/?* (o-u)

Repeat this process with the pictures in the remaining rows. Students may be aware that **ow** can also stand for the **long o** sound. If they have difficulty decoding words spelled with **ow**, tell them to try sounding out the word with both /ō/ and /ou/ to see which sound makes a familiar word.

2. Read and Understand ....

Have students turn over their mats. Distribute the task cards for Mat B. Explain that this mat has two sections: one for words with the /oi/ sound as in **voyage** and one for words with the /ou/ sound as in **cloud**. Then show the task card that has a picture of a monster destroying a town and say:

*The picture on this card shows a monster destroying a town. Do you hear /oi/ or /ou/ in the word **destroy**? (/oi/) That's right;* **destroy** *has the sound of /oi/ as in* **voyage***, so I'll place this card in that section of the mat.*

Repeat this process with the remaining task cards. If your students are capable, have them tell you the names of the pictures rather than you saying them. (coins, soil, boy; mouth, frown, pounds, crowd)

3. Practice the Skill ....

Distribute the Practice It! activity (page 121) to students. Read the directions aloud and have students read the words below the pictures. Then say:

Let's blend the sounds to read word number 1: /r/ /oi/ /l/ royal. Do you hear /oi/ or /ou/ in **royal**? (/oi/) *Do you hear /oi/ in* **poison** *or in* **pounds**? (poison) *Now draw a line from the word* **royal** *to the picture of poison.*

Repeat this process for the remaining words.

Apply and Assess

After the lesson, distribute the Read It! activity (page 122) to students and read the directions aloud. Have students complete the activity independently. Then listen to them read the sentences. Use the results as an informal assessment of students' skill mastery.

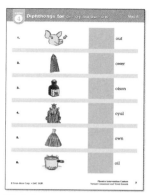

Mat A

Mat B

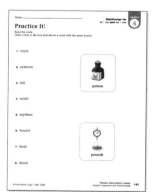

Page 121

Page 122

oi • oy

noise

enj<u>oy</u>

EMC 3528
Center 4 • Sound Card

ou • ow

<u>lou</u>d

<u>ow</u>l

EMC 3528
Center 4 • Sound Card

Answer Keys

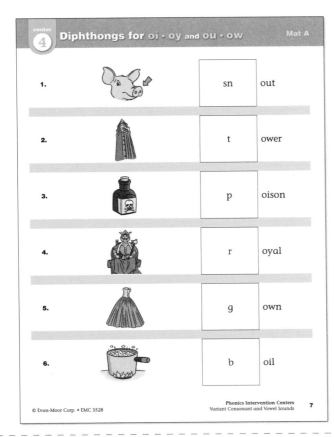

pouch
sound
tower

Center 4 • Sound Card

boys
joint
coil

Center 4 • Sound Card

Answer Keys

Name _____

Diphthongs for
oi • oy and ou • ow

center 4

Practice It!

Read the word.
Draw a line to the box that shows a word with the same sound.

1. royal
2. eyebrow
3. foil
4. south
5. soybean
6. hound
7. broil
8. shout

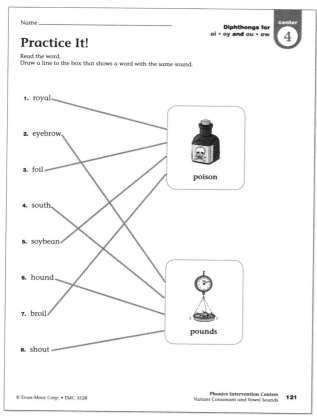

poison

pounds

© Evan-Moor Corp. • EMC 3528

Phonics Intervention Centers
Variant Consonant and Vowel Sounds **121**

Name _____

Diphthongs for
oi • oy and ou • ow

center 4

Read It!

Write the two words on the correct lines to complete each sentence.

1. couch   mouse
   A brown **mouse** just ran under the **couch** !

2. noise   toys
   Most little boys like **toys** that make **noise** .

3. destroy   town
   A tornado can **destroy** an entire **town** !

4. cowboy   down
   The **cowboy** rode his horse **down** the trail.

5. coins   pouch
   Wow! Roy found a **pouch** full of gold **coins** !

6. moist   sprout
   You must keep seeds **moist** so they will **sprout** .

7. soil   snout
   The pig stuck its **snout** in the **soil** .

8. annoy   voices
   Loud **voices** **annoy** me sometimes.

122 **Phonics Intervention Centers**
Variant Consonant and Vowel Sounds

EMC 3528 • © Evan-Moor Corp.

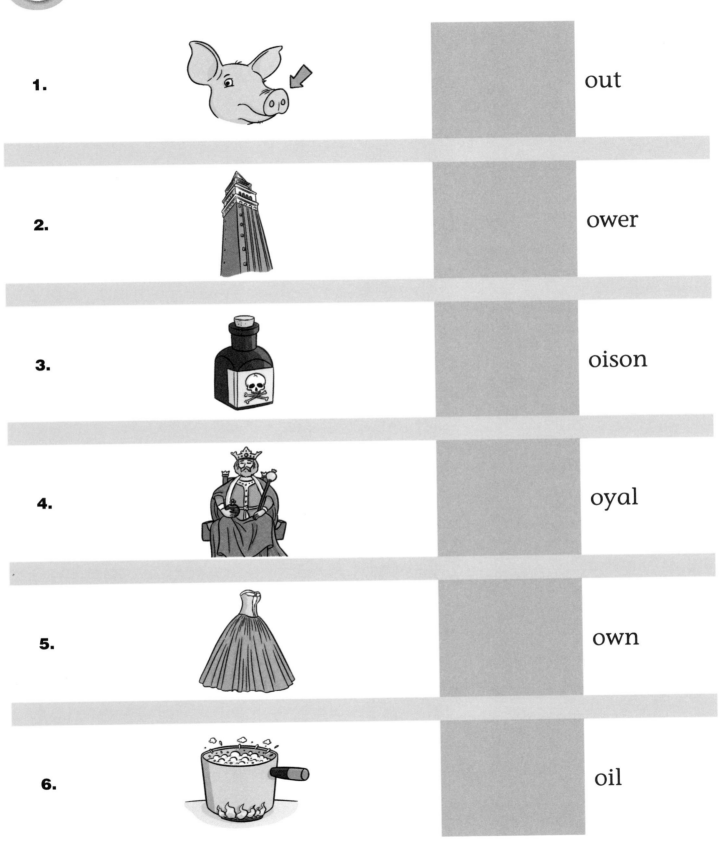

1.   out

2.   ower

3.   oison

4.   oyal

5.   own

6.   oil

oi • oy

voyage

ou • ow

cloud

1. out

2. ower

3. oison

4. oyal

5. own

6. oil

oi • oy

voyage

---

ou • ow

cloud

Phonics Intervention Centers
Variant Consonant and Vowel Sounds

EMC 3528 • © Evan-Moor Corp.

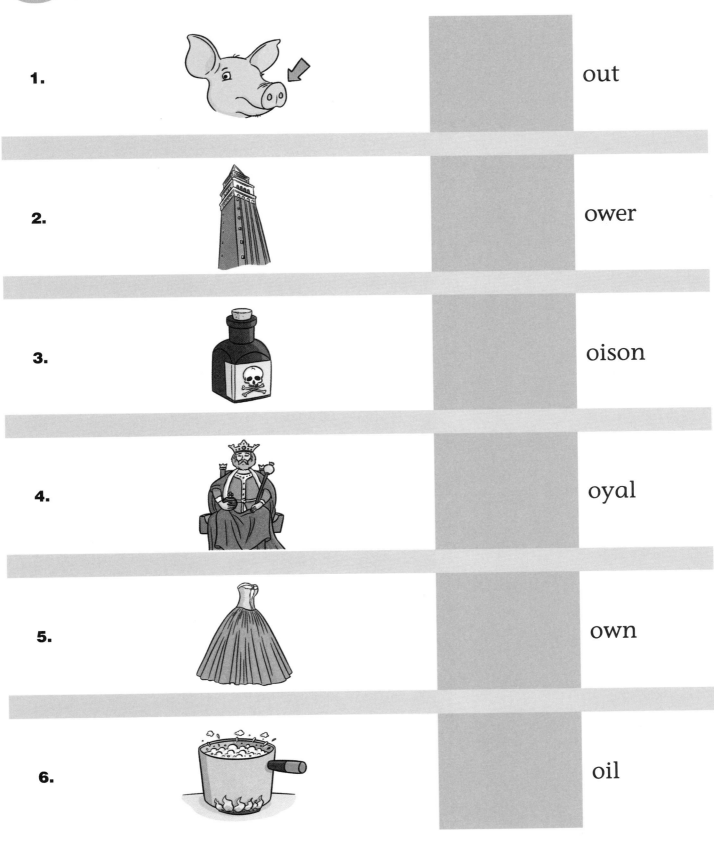

1. out

2. ower

3. oison

4. oyal

5. own

6. oil

oi · oy

voyage

ou · ow

cloud

Phonics Intervention Centers
Variant Consonant and Vowel Sounds

EMC 3528 • © Evan-Moor Corp.

1.

out

2.

ower

3.

oison

4.

oyal

5.

own

6.

oil

oi • oy

voyage

ou • ow

cloud

Phonics Intervention Centers
Variant Consonant and Vowel Sounds

EMC 3528 • © Evan-Moor Corp.

1.

out

2.

ower

3.

oison

4.

oyal

5.

own

6.

oil

oi • oy

voyage

ou • ow

cloud

1.   out

2.   ower

3.   oison

4.   oyal

5.   own

6.   oil

oi • oy

voyage

ou • ow

cloud

Student 1	Student 2	Student 3	Student 4	Student 5	Student 6
b	b	b	b	b	b
p	p	p	p	p	p
g	g	g	g	g	g
r	r	r	r	r	r
sn	sn	sn	sn	sn	sn
t	t	t	t	t	t

Student 6

EMC 3528
Center 4 • Mat A

Student 6

EMC 3528
Center 4 • Mat A

Student 6

EMC 3528
Center 4 • Mat A

Student 6

EMC 3528
Center 4 • Mat A

Student 6

EMC 3528
Center 4 • Mat A

Student 6

EMC 3528
Center 4 • Mat A

Student 5

EMC 3528
Center 4 • Mat A

Student 5

EMC 3528
Center 4 • Mat A

Student 5

EMC 3528
Center 4 • Mat A

Student 5

EMC 3528
Center 4 • Mat A

Student 5

EMC 3528
Center 4 • Mat A

Student 5

EMC 3528
Center 4 • Mat A

Student 4

EMC 3528
Center 4 • Mat A

Student 4

EMC 3528
Center 4 • Mat A

Student 4

EMC 3528
Center 4 • Mat A

Student 4

EMC 3528
Center 4 • Mat A

Student 4

EMC 3528
Center 4 • Mat A

Student 4

EMC 3528
Center 4 • Mat A

Student 3

EMC 3528
Center 4 • Mat A

Student 3

EMC 3528
Center 4 • Mat A

Student 3

EMC 3528
Center 4 • Mat A

Student 3

EMC 3528
Center 4 • Mat A

Student 3

EMC 3528
Center 4 • Mat A

Student 3

EMC 3528
Center 4 • Mat A

Student 2

EMC 3528
Center 4 • Mat A

Student 2

EMC 3528
Center 4 • Mat A

Student 2

EMC 3528
Center 4 • Mat A

Student 2

EMC 3528
Center 4 • Mat A

Student 2

EMC 3528
Center 4 • Mat A

Student 2

EMC 3528
Center 4 • Mat A

Student 1

EMC 3528
Center 4 • Mat A

Student 1

EMC 3528
Center 4 • Mat A

Student 1

EMC 3528
Center 4 • Mat A

Student 1

EMC 3528
Center 4 • Mat A

Student 1

EMC 3528
Center 4 • Mat A

Student 1

EMC 3528
Center 4 • Mat A

Phonics Intervention Centers
Variant Consonant and Vowel Sounds

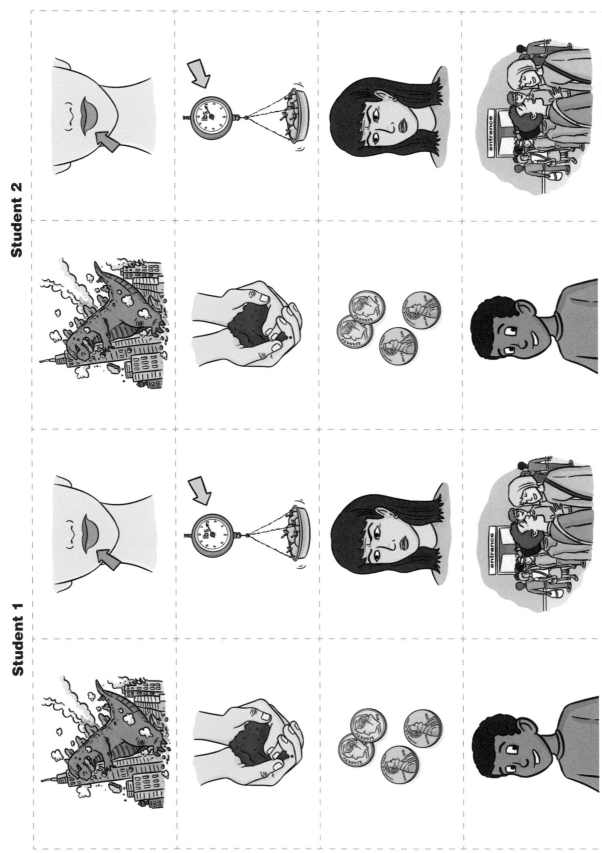

Student 2

Student 1

Phonics Intervention Centers
Variant Consonant and Vowel Sounds

Student 2

EMC 3528 • Center 4 • Mat B

Student 2

EMC 3528 • Center 4 • Mat B

Student 2

EMC 3528 • Center 4 • Mat B

Student 2

EMC 3528 • Center 4 • Mat B

Student 2

EMC 3528 • Center 4 • Mat B

Student 2

EMC 3528 • Center 4 • Mat B

Student 2

EMC 3528 • Center 4 • Mat B

Student 2

EMC 3528 • Center 4 • Mat B

Student 1

EMC 3528 • Center 4 • Mat B

Student 1

EMC 3528 • Center 4 • Mat B

Student 1

EMC 3528 • Center 4 • Mat B

Student 1

EMC 3528 • Center 4 • Mat B

Student 1

EMC 3528 • Center 4 • Mat B

Student 1

EMC 3528 • Center 4 • Mat B

Student 1

EMC 3528 • Center 4 • Mat B

Student 1

EMC 3528 • Center 4 • Mat B

Student 4

Student 3

Student 4

EMC 3528 • Center 4 • Mat B

Student 4

EMC 3528 • Center 4 • Mat B

Student 4

EMC 3528 • Center 4 • Mat B

Student 4

EMC 3528 • Center 4 • Mat B

Student 4

EMC 3528 • Center 4 • Mat B

Student 4

EMC 3528 • Center 4 • Mat B

Student 3

EMC 3528 • Center 4 • Mat B

Student 3

EMC 3528 • Center 4 • Mat B

Student 3

EMC 3528 • Center 4 • Mat B

Student 3

EMC 3528 • Center 4 • Mat B

Student 3

EMC 3528 • Center 4 • Mat B

Student 3

EMC 3528 • Center 4 • Mat B

Student 6

EMC 3528 • Center 4 • Mat B

Student 6

EMC 3528 • Center 4 • Mat B

Student 6

EMC 3528 • Center 4 • Mat B

Student 6

EMC 3528 • Center 4 • Mat B

Student 6

EMC 3528 • Center 4 • Mat B

Student 6

EMC 3528 • Center 4 • Mat B

Student 6

EMC 3528 • Center 4 • Mat B

Student 6

EMC 3528 • Center 4 • Mat B

Student 5

EMC 3528 • Center 4 • Mat B

Student 5

EMC 3528 • Center 4 • Mat B

Student 5

EMC 3528 • Center 4 • Mat B

Student 5

EMC 3528 • Center 4 • Mat B

Student 5

EMC 3528 • Center 4 • Mat B

Student 5

EMC 3528 • Center 4 • Mat B

Student 5

EMC 3528 • Center 4 • Mat B

Student 5

EMC 3528 • Center 4 • Mat B

Practice It!

Read the word.
Draw a line to the box that shows a word with the same sound.

1. royal

2. eyebrow

3. foil

4. south

5. soybean

6. hound

7. broil

8. shout

poison

pounds

Name _____

Read It!

Write the two words on the correct lines to complete each sentence.

1. (couch   mouse)

A brown _____ just ran under the _____!

2. (noise   toys)

Most little boys like _____ that make _____.

3. (destroy   town)

A tornado can _____ an entire _____!

4. (cowboy   down)

The _____ rode his horse _____ the trail.

5. (coins   pouch)

Wow! Roy found a _____ full of gold _____!

6. (moist   sprout)

You must keep seeds _____ so they will _____.

7. (soil   snout)

The pig stuck its _____ in the _____.

8. (annoy   voices)

Loud _____ _____ me sometimes.

center

5

Two Sounds of c

For the Teacher

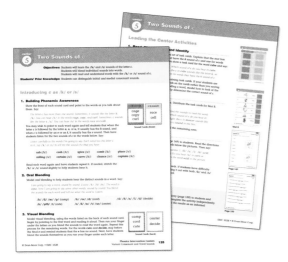

Lesson Plan

c (k sound)

cage
copy
curl

camp
cord
cute

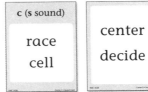

c (s sound)

race
cell

center
decide

Sound Cards

Answer Keys

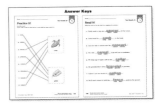

Answer Keys

For the Student

front (Mat A)

back (Mat B)

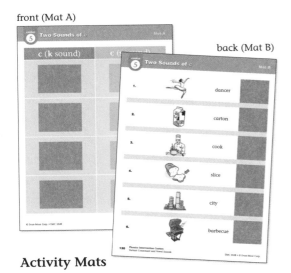

Activity Mats

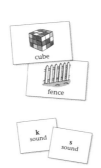

Task Cards

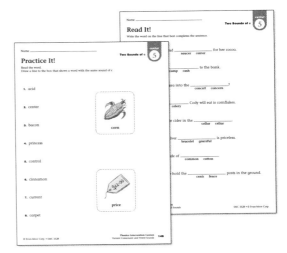

Practice and Assessment Activities

Two Sounds of c

Objectives: Students will learn the **/k/** and **/s/** sounds of the letter *c*.
Students will blend individual sounds into words.
Students will read and understand words with the **/k/** or **/s/** sound of *c*.

Students' Prior Knowledge: Students can distinguish initial and medial consonant sounds.

Introducing *c* as /k/ or /s/

1. Building Phonemic Awareness

Show the front of each sound card and point to the words as you talk about them. Say:

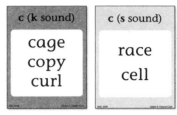

Sound Cards (front)

*The letter **c** has more than one sound. Sometimes, it sounds like the letter **k**: /k/. You can hear /k/ in the words **cage**, **copy**, and **curl**. Sometimes, c sounds like the letter **s**: /s/. You can hear /s/ in the words **race** and **cell**.*

You may wish to point to each word again and tell students that when the letter *c* is followed by the letter *a*, *o*, or *u*, it usually has the *k* sound, and when *c* is followed by an *e* or an *i*, it usually has the *s* sound. Then have students listen for the two sounds of *c* in the words below. Say:

*Listen carefully to the words I'm going to say. Each word has the letter **c** in it. Say /k/ or /s/ to tell me the sound of c that you hear.*

cab (/k/)	**cash** (/k/)	**spice** (/s/)	**comb** (/k/)	**place** (/s/)
ceiling (/s/)	**certain** (/s/)	**curve** (/k/)	**chance** (/s/)	**captain** (/k/)

Read each word again and have students repeat it. If needed, stretch the **/k/** or **/s/** sound slightly to help students hear it.

2. Oral Blending

Model oral blending to help students hear the distinct sounds in a word. Say:

*I am going to say a word, sound by sound. Listen: /k/ /ō/ /n/. The word is **cone**. Now I am going to say some other words, sound by sound. You blend the sounds for each word and tell me what the word is. Listen:*

/k/ /ă/ /m/ /p/ (camp)	/k/ /or/ /d/ (cord)	/d/ /ē/ /s/ /ī/ /d/ (decide)
/k/ /yōō/ /t/ (cute)	/s/ /ĕ/ /n/ /t/ /ur/ (center)	

3. Visual Blending

Model visual blending, using the words listed on the back of each sound card. Begin by pointing to the first word and reading it aloud. Then run your finger under the letters as you blend the sounds to read the word again. Repeat this process for the remaining words. For the words **cute** and **decide**, stop before the final *e* and remind students that the *e* has no sound. Next, have students blend the sounds themselves as you run your finger under each letter.

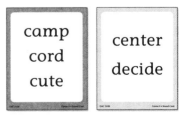

Sound Cards (back)

center 5

Two Sounds of c (continued)

Leading the Center Activities

1. Read, Discriminate, and Identify ....

Give each student Mat A and a set of task cards. Explain that the mat has two columns: one for words that have the **k** sound of **c** and one for words that have the **s** sound of **c**. Then show a task card for the word **cube** and say:

*The word on this card is **cube**. Which sound of c do you hear in **cube**: /k/ or /s/? (/k/) That's right; the c in **cube** sounds like the letter k, so I'll place this card in the column for words that have the k sound of c.*

Repeat this process with the remaining task cards. If your students are capable, have them read the words on the cards rather than you saying them. If they have difficulty decoding a word, model how to look at the letter that comes after the **c** to help determine the correct sound of **c**.

2. Read and Understand ....

Have students turn over their mats. Distribute the task cards for Mat B. Then say:

*Look at the word in row 1. Let's blend the sounds to read the word: /d/ /ă/ /n/ /s/ /ur/ **dancer**. Which sound of c do you hear in **dancer**: /k/ or /s/? (/s/) That's right; the c in **dancer** sounds like the letter s, so place a card that says **s sound** in the box.*

Repeat this process with the words in the remaining rows.

3. Practice the Skill ....

Distribute the Practice It! activity (page 149) to students. Read the directions aloud and have students read the words below the pictures. Then say:

*Let's blend the sounds to read word number 1: /ă/ /s/ /ĭ/ /d/ **acid**. Do you hear /k/ or /s/ in **acid**? (/s/) Do you hear /s/ in **corn** or in **price**? (price) Now draw a line from the word **acid** to the picture of the price tag.*

Repeat this process for the remaining words. If students have difficulty decoding a word, tell them to try sounding it out with both /k/ and /s/ to see which sound makes a familiar word.

Apply and Assess

After the lesson, distribute the Read It! activity (page 150) to students and read the directions aloud. Have students complete the activity independently. Then listen to them read the sentences. Use the results as an informal assessment of students' skill mastery.

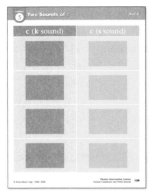

Mat A

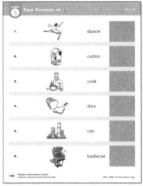

Mat B

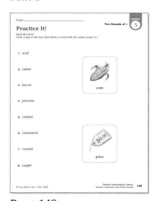

Page 149

Page 150

126 **Phonics Intervention Centers**
Variant Consonant and Vowel Sounds

EMC 3528 • © Evan-Moor Corp.

c (k sound)

cage
copy
curl

EMC 3528 Center 5 • Sound Card

c (s sound)

race
cell

EMC 3528 Center 5 • Sound Card

Answer Keys

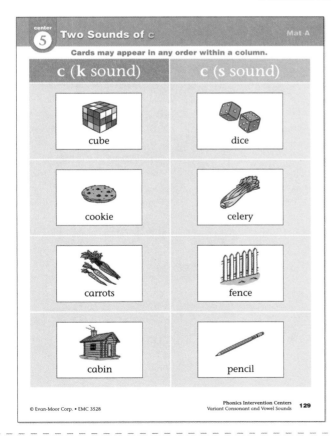

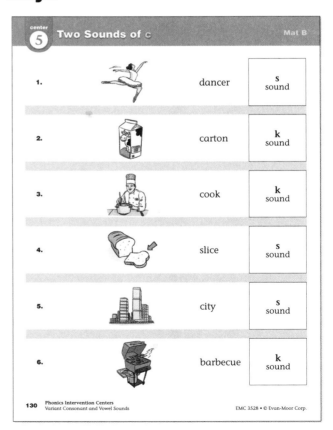

center

decide

camp

cord

cute

Answer Keys

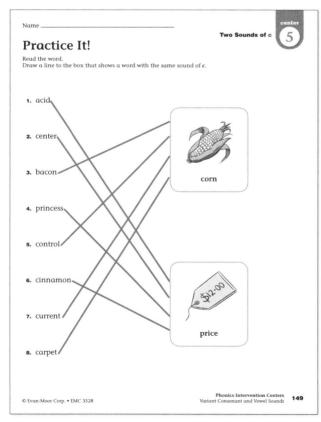

Name _____

Two Sounds of c   center 5

Practice It!

Read the word.
Draw a line to the box that shows a word with the same sound of **c**.

1. acid
2. center
3. bacon
4. princess
5. control
6. cinnamon
7. current
8. carpet

corn

price

$12.00

© Evan-Moor Corp. • EMC 3528

Phonics Intervention Centers
Variant Consonant and Vowel Sounds   **149**

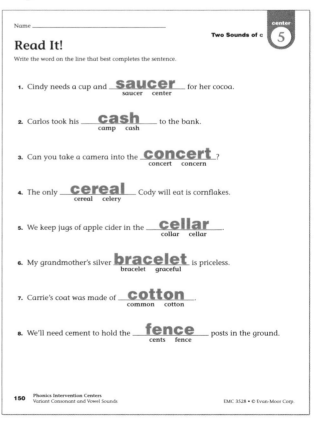

Name _____

Two Sounds of c   center 5

Read It!

Write the word on the line that best completes the sentence.

1. Cindy needs a cup and **saucer** for her cocoa.
   saucer   center

2. Carlos took his **cash** to the bank.
   camp   cash

3. Can you take a camera into the **concert** ?
   concert   concern

4. The only **cereal** Cody will eat is cornflakes.
   cereal   celery

5. We keep jugs of apple cider in the **cellar** .
   collar   cellar

6. My grandmother's silver **bracelet** is priceless.
   bracelet   graceful

7. Carrie's coat was made of **cotton** .
   common   cotton

8. We'll need cement to hold the **fence** posts in the ground.
   cents   fence

150   Phonics Intervention Centers
Variant Consonant and Vowel Sounds

EMC 3528 • © Evan-Moor Corp.

c (k sound)	c (s sound)

1. dancer

2. carton

3. cook

4. slice

5. city

6. barbecue

c (k sound)

c (s sound)

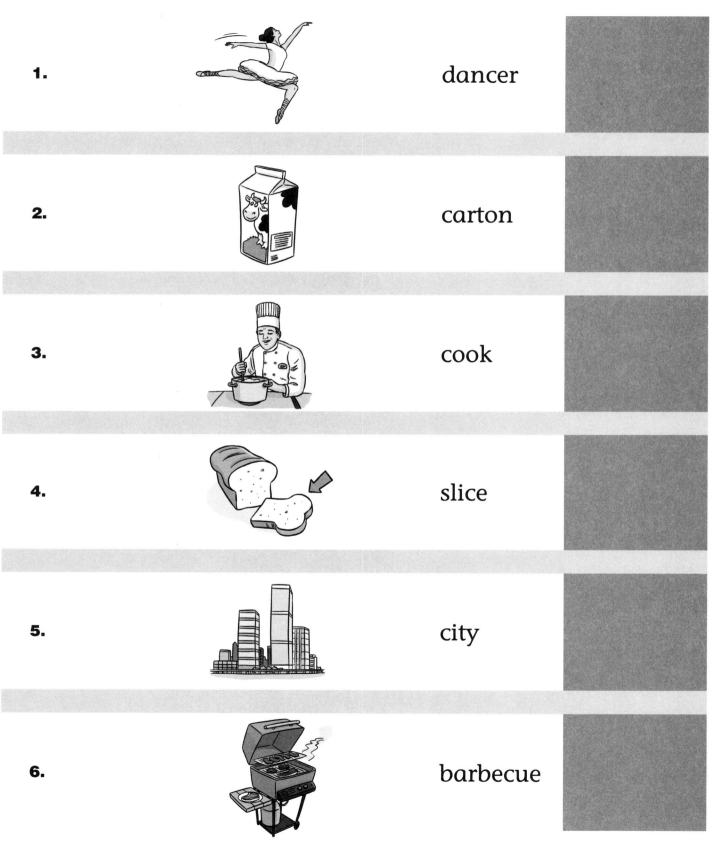

1. dancer

2. carton

3. cook

4. slice

5. city

6. barbecue

c (k sound)	c (s sound)

1. dancer

2. carton

3. cook

4. slice

5. city

6. barbecue

Phonics Intervention Centers
Variant Consonant and Vowel Sounds

c (k sound)

c (s sound)

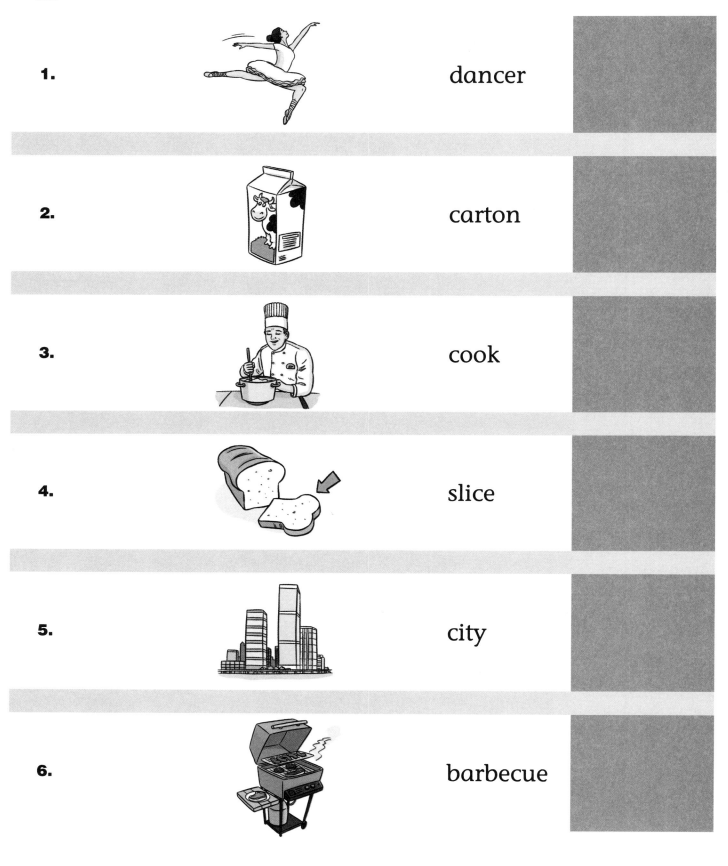

1. dancer

2. carton

3. cook

4. slice

5. city

6. barbecue

c (k sound)	c (s sound)

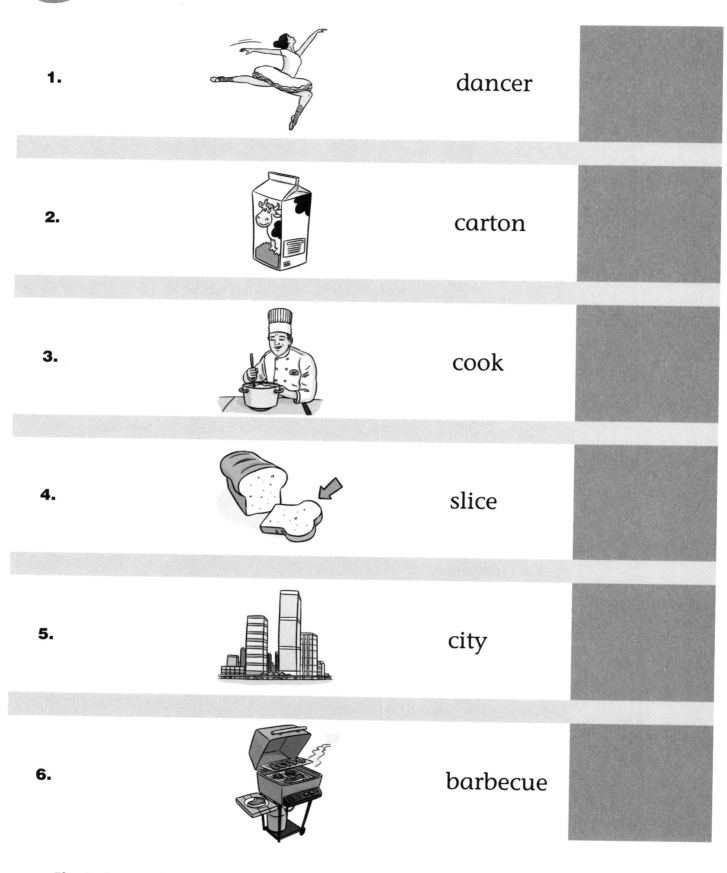

1. dancer

2. carton

3. cook

4. slice

5. city

6. barbecue

c (k sound)	c (s sound)

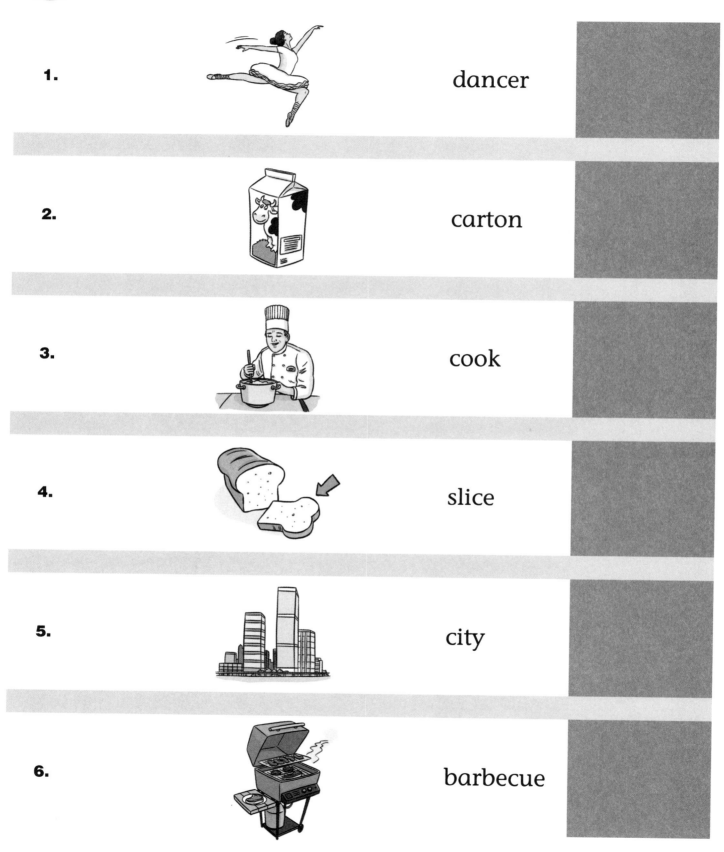

1. dancer

2. carton

3. cook

4. slice

5. city

6. barbecue

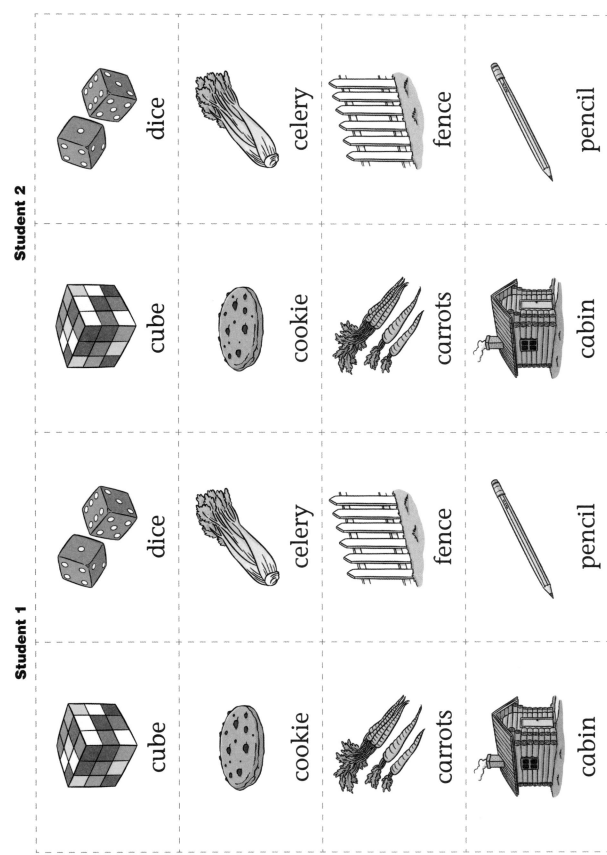

Student 2

dice

celery

fence

pencil

cube

cookie

carrots

cabin

Student 1

dice

celery

fence

pencil

cube

cookie

carrots

cabin

Student 2

EMC 3528 • Center 5 • Mat A

Student 2

EMC 3528 • Center 5 • Mat A

Student 2

EMC 3528 • Center 5 • Mat A

Student 2

EMC 3528 • Center 5 • Mat A

Student 2

EMC 3528 • Center 5 • Mat A

Student 2

EMC 3528 • Center 5 • Mat A

Student 2

EMC 3528 • Center 5 • Mat A

Student 2

EMC 3528 • Center 5 • Mat A

Student 1

EMC 3528 • Center 5 • Mat A

Student 1

EMC 3528 • Center 5 • Mat A

Student 1

EMC 3528 • Center 5 • Mat A

Student 1

EMC 3528 • Center 5 • Mat A

Student 1

EMC 3528 • Center 5 • Mat A

Student 1

EMC 3528 • Center 5 • Mat A

Student 1

EMC 3528 • Center 5 • Mat A

Student 1

EMC 3528 • Center 5 • Mat A

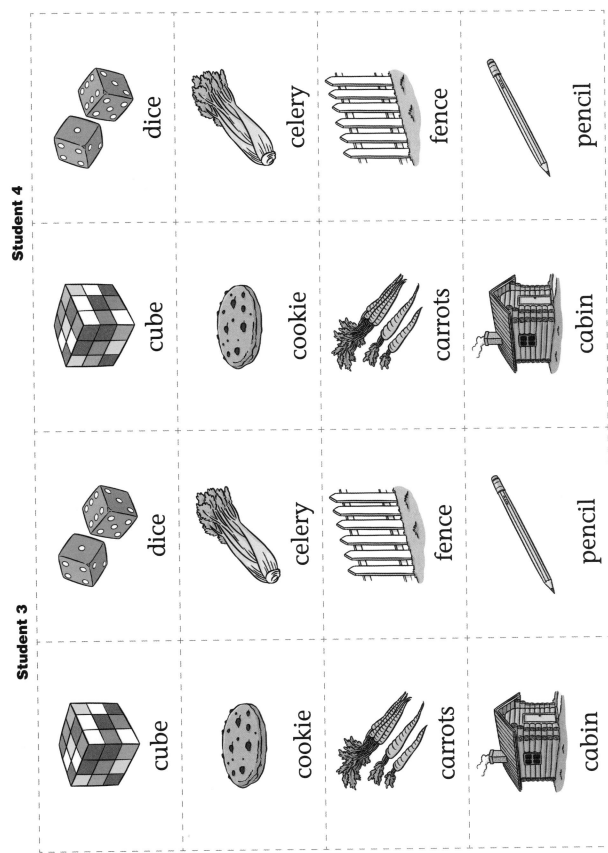

Student 4

dice

celery

fence

pencil

cube

cookie

carrots

cabin

Student 3

dice

celery

fence

pencil

cube

cookie

carrots

cabin

Student 4

EMC 3528 • Center 5 • Mat A

Student 4

EMC 3528 • Center 5 • Mat A

Student 4

EMC 3528 • Center 5 • Mat A

Student 4

EMC 3528 • Center 5 • Mat A

Student 4

EMC 3528 • Center 5 • Mat A

Student 4

EMC 3528 • Center 5 • Mat A

Student 4

EMC 3528 • Center 5 • Mat A

Student 3

EMC 3528 • Center 5 • Mat A

Student 3

EMC 3528 • Center 5 • Mat A

Student 3

EMC 3528 • Center 5 • Mat A

Student 3

EMC 3528 • Center 5 • Mat A

Student 3

EMC 3528 • Center 5 • Mat A

Student 3

EMC 3528 • Center 5 • Mat A

Student 3

EMC 3528 • Center 5 • Mat A

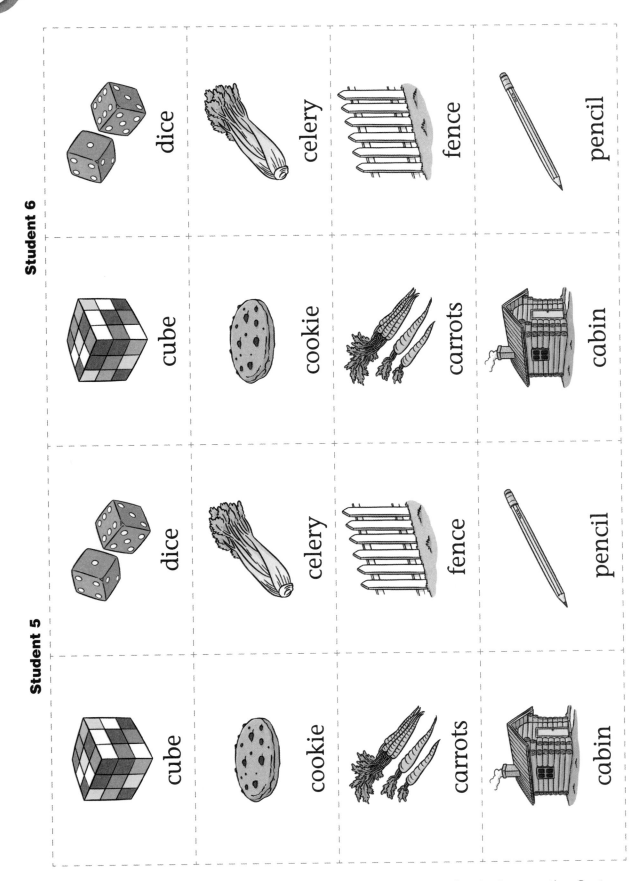

Student 6

dice

celery

fence

pencil

cube

cookie

carrots

cabin

Student 5

dice

celery

fence

pencil

cube

cookie

carrots

cabin

Student 6

EMC 3528 • Center 5 • Mat A

Student 6

EMC 3528 • Center 5 • Mat A

Student 6

EMC 3528 • Center 5 • Mat A

Student 6

EMC 3528 • Center 5 • Mat A

Student 6

EMC 3528 • Center 5 • Mat A

Student 6

EMC 3528 • Center 5 • Mat A

Student 6

EMC 3528 • Center 5 • Mat A

Student 5

EMC 3528 • Center 5 • Mat A

Student 5

EMC 3528 • Center 5 • Mat A

Student 5

EMC 3528 • Center 5 • Mat A

Student 5

EMC 3528 • Center 5 • Mat A

Student 5

EMC 3528 • Center 5 • Mat A

Student 5

EMC 3528 • Center 5 • Mat A

Student 5

EMC 3528 • Center 5 • Mat A

Student 1	Student 2	Student 3	Student 4	Student 5	Student 6
k sound	**k** sound	**k** sound	**k** sound	**k** sound	**k** sound
k sound	**k** sound	**k** sound	**k** sound	**k** sound	**k** sound
k sound	**k** sound	**k** sound	**k** sound	**k** sound	**k** sound
s sound	**s** sound	**s** sound	**s** sound	**s** sound	**s** sound
s sound	**s** sound	**s** sound	**s** sound	**s** sound	**s** sound
s sound	**s** sound	**s** sound	**s** sound	**s** sound	**s** sound

Student 6 — EMC 3528 Center 5 • Mat B
Student 6 — EMC 3528 Center 5 • Mat B
Student 6 — EMC 3528 Center 5 • Mat B
Student 6 — EMC 3528 Center 5 • Mat B
Student 6 — EMC 3528 Center 5 • Mat B
Student 6 — EMC 3528 Center 5 • Mat B

Student 5 — EMC 3528 Center 5 • Mat B
Student 5 — EMC 3528 Center 5 • Mat B
Student 5 — EMC 3528 Center 5 • Mat B
Student 5 — EMC 3528 Center 5 • Mat B
Student 5 — EMC 3528 Center 5 • Mat B
Student 5 — EMC 3528 Center 5 • Mat B

Student 4 — EMC 3528 Center 5 • Mat B
Student 4 — EMC 3528 Center 5 • Mat B
Student 4 — EMC 3528 Center 5 • Mat B
Student 4 — EMC 3528 Center 5 • Mat B
Student 4 — EMC 3528 Center 5 • Mat B
Student 4 — EMC 3528 Center 5 • Mat B

Student 3 — EMC 3528 Center 5 • Mat B
Student 3 — EMC 3528 Center 5 • Mat B
Student 3 — EMC 3528 Center 5 • Mat B
Student 3 — EMC 3528 Center 5 • Mat B
Student 3 — EMC 3528 Center 5 • Mat B
Student 3 — EMC 3528 Center 5 • Mat B

Student 2 — EMC 3528 Center 5 • Mat B
Student 2 — EMC 3528 Center 5 • Mat B
Student 2 — EMC 3528 Center 5 • Mat B
Student 2 — EMC 3528 Center 5 • Mat B
Student 2 — EMC 3528 Center 5 • Mat B
Student 2 — EMC 3528 Center 5 • Mat B

Student 1 — EMC 3528 Center 5 • Mat B
Student 1 — EMC 3528 Center 5 • Mat B
Student 1 — EMC 3528 Center 5 • Mat B
Student 1 — EMC 3528 Center 5 • Mat B
Student 1 — EMC 3528 Center 5 • Mat B
Student 1 — EMC 3528 Center 5 • Mat B

Practice It!

Read the word.
Draw a line to the box that shows a word with the same sound of *c*.

1. acid

2. center

3. bacon

4. princess

5. control

6. cinnamon

7. current

8. carpet

corn

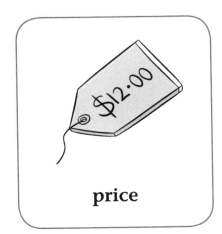

price

Name _____

Read It!

Write the word on the line that best completes the sentence.

1. Cindy needs a cup and _____ for her cocoa.
saucer   center

2. Carlos took his _____ to the bank.
camp   cash

3. Can you take a camera into the _____?
concert   concern

4. The only _____ Cody will eat is cornflakes.
cereal   celery

5. We keep jugs of apple cider in the _____.
collar   cellar

6. My grandmother's silver _____ is priceless.
bracelet   graceful

7. Carrie's coat was made of _____.
common   cotton

8. We'll need cement to hold the _____ posts in the ground.
cents   fence

Two Sounds of **g**

For the Teacher

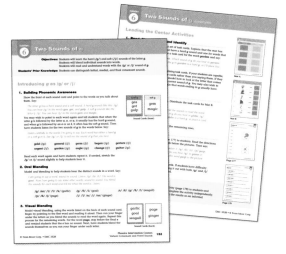

Lesson Plan

Sound Cards

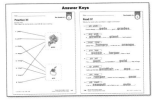

Answer Keys

For the Student

front (Mat A)

back (Mat B)

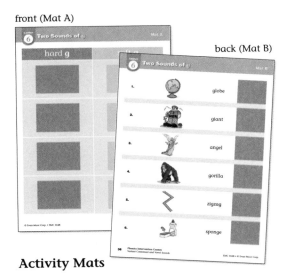

Activity Mats

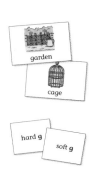

Task Cards

Practice and Assessment Activities

Two Sounds of g

Objectives: Students will learn the hard (/g/) and soft (/j/) sounds of the letter **g**.
Students will blend individual sounds into words.
Students will read and understand words with the /g/ or /j/ sound of **g**.

Students' Prior Knowledge: Students can distinguish initial, medial, and final consonant sounds.

Introducing g as /g/ or /j/

1. Building Phonemic Awareness

Show the front of each sound card and point to the words as you talk about them. Say:

*The letter **g** has a hard sound and a soft sound. A hard **g** sounds like this: /g/. You can hear /g/ in the words **gas**, **got**, and **gulp**. A soft **g** sounds like the letter **j**: /j/. You can hear /j/ in the words **gem** and **magic**.*

Sound Cards (front)

You may wish to point to each word again and tell students that when the letter **g** is followed by the letter **a**, **o**, or **u**, it usually has the hard **g** sound, and when **g** is followed by an **e** or an **i**, it often has the soft **g** sound. Then have students listen for the two sounds of **g** in the words below. Say:

*Listen carefully to the words I'm going to say. Each word has either a hard **g** or a soft **g** in it. Say /g/ or /j/ to tell me the sound of **g** that you hear.*

gold (/g/)	**general** (/j/)	**germ** (/j/)	**began** (/g/)	**gesture** (/j/)
urgent (/j/)	**garden** (/g/)	**eagle** (/g/)	**change** (/j/)	**guitar** (/g/)

Read each word again and have students repeat it. If needed, stretch the /g/ or /j/ sound slightly to help students hear it.

2. Oral Blending

Model oral blending to help students hear the distinct sounds in a word. Say:

*I am going to say a word, sound by sound. Listen: /g/ /ō/ /t/. The word is **goat**. Now I am going to say some other words, sound by sound. You blend the sounds for each word and tell me what the word is. Listen:*

/g/ /ar/ /l/ /ĭ/ /k/ (garlic)	/g/ /ō/ /l/ (goal)	/s/ /ē/ /g/ /ŭ/ /l/ (seagull)
/p/ /ā/ /j/ (page)	/j/ /ĭ/ /n/ /j/ /ur/ (ginger)	

3. Visual Blending

Model visual blending, using the words listed on the back of each sound card. Begin by pointing to the first word and reading it aloud. Then run your finger under the letters as you blend the sounds to read the word again. Repeat this process for the remaining words. For the word **page**, stop before the final **e** and remind students that the **e** has no sound. Next, have students blend the sounds themselves as you run your finger under each letter.

Sound Cards (back)

Leading the Center Activities

1. Read, Discriminate, and Identify

Give each student Mat A and a set of task cards. Explain that the mat has two columns: one for words that have a hard **g** sound and one for words that have a soft **g** sound. Then show a task card for the word **garden** and say:

*The word on this card is **garden**. Which sound of **g** do you hear in **garden**: /g/ or /j/? (/g/) That's right; the **g** in **garden** is a hard **g**, so I'll place this card under **hard g** on the mat.*

Repeat this process with the remaining task cards. If your students are capable, have them read the words on the cards rather than you saying them. If they have difficulty decoding a word, model how to look at the letter that comes after the **g** to help determine the correct sound of **g**. You may also wish to point to the word **plug** and explain that words ending in **g** usually have the /g/ sound.

2. Read and Understand

Have students turn over their mats. Distribute the task cards for Mat B. Then say:

*Look at the word in row 1. Let's blend the sounds to read the word: /gl/ /ō/ /b/ **globe**. Which sound of **g** do you hear in **globe**: /g/ or /j/? (/g/) That's right; the **g** in **globe** is a hard **g**, so place a card that says **hard g** in the box.*

Repeat this process with the words in the remaining rows.

3. Practice the Skill

Distribute the Practice It! activity (page 177) to students. Read the directions aloud and have students read the words below the pictures. Then say:

*Let's blend the sounds to read word number 1: /g/ /ă/ /s/ /p/ **gasp**. Do you hear /g/ or /j/ in **gasp**? (/g/) Do you hear /g/ in **game** or in **gem**? (game) Now draw a line from the word **gasp** to the picture of the game.*

Repeat this process for the remaining words. If students have difficulty decoding a word, tell them to try sounding it out with both /g/ and /j/ to see which sound makes a familiar word.

Apply and Assess

After the lesson, distribute the Read It! activity (page 178) to students and read the directions aloud. Have students complete the activity independently. Then listen to them read the sentences. Use the results as an informal assessment of students' skill mastery.

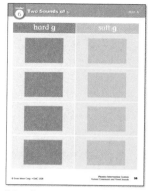

Mat A

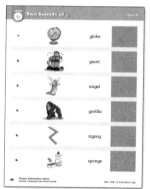

Mat B

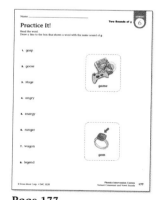

Page 177

Page 178

hard **g**

gas
got
gulp

EMC 3528

Center 6 • Sound Card

soft **g**

gem
magic

EMC 3528

Center 6 • Sound Card

Answer Keys

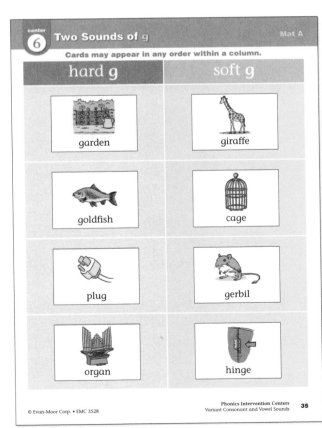

page

ginger

garlic

goal

seagull

Answer Keys

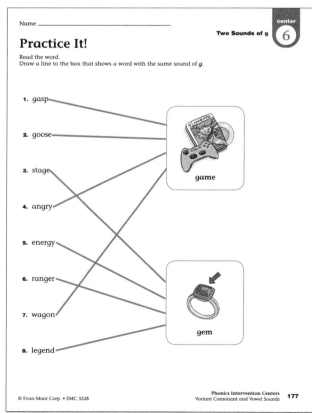

Name _____

Practice It!

Two Sounds of g — center 6

Read the word.
Draw a line to the box that shows a word with the same sound of *g*.

1. gasp
2. goose
3. stage
4. angry
5. energy
6. ranger
7. wagon
8. legend

game

gem

© Evan-Moor Corp. • EMC 3528   Phonics Intervention Centers
Variant Consonant and Vowel Sounds   **177**

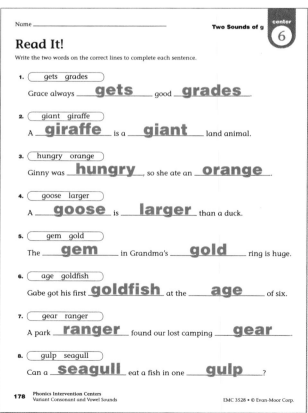

Name _____

Read It!

Two Sounds of g — center 6

Write the two words on the correct lines to complete each sentence.

1. (gets grades)
Grace always **gets** good **grades**.

2. (giant giraffe)
A **giraffe** is a **giant** land animal.

3. (hungry orange)
Ginny was **hungry**, so she ate an **orange**.

4. (goose larger)
A **goose** is **larger** than a duck.

5. (gem gold)
The **gem** in Grandma's **gold** ring is huge.

6. (age goldfish)
Gabe got his first **goldfish** at the **age** of six.

7. (gear ranger)
A park **ranger** found our lost camping **gear**.

8. (gulp seagull)
Can a **seagull** eat a fish in one **gulp**?

178 Phonics Intervention Centers
Variant Consonant and Vowel Sounds   EMC 3528 • © Evan-Moor Corp.

hard **g**	soft **g**

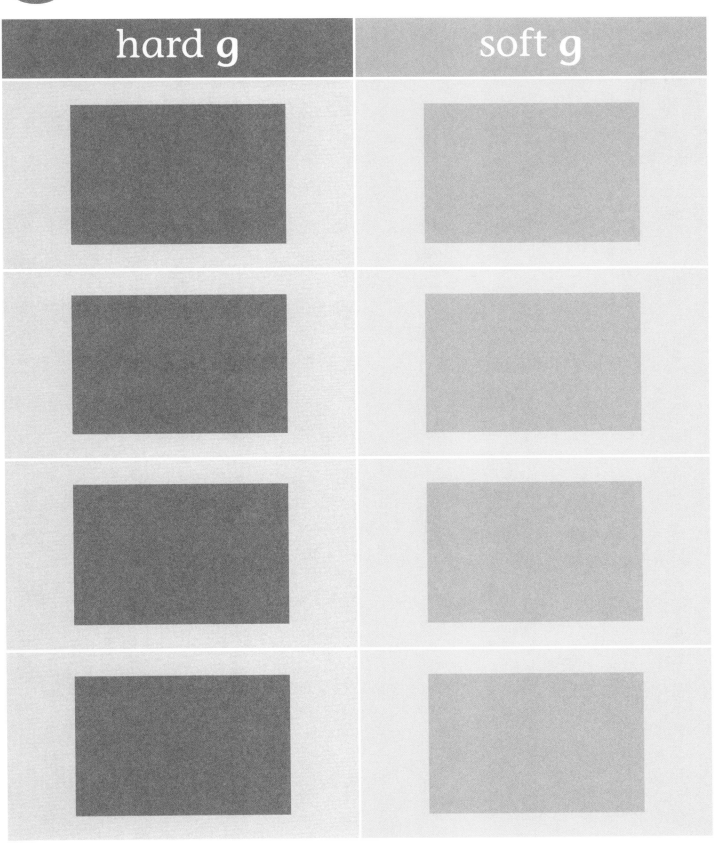

1. globe

2. giant

3. angel

4. gorilla

5. zigzag

6. sponge

Phonics Intervention Centers
Variant Consonant and Vowel Sounds

EMC 3528 • © Evan-Moor Corp.

hard **g**	soft **g**

1.

globe

2.

giant

3.

angel

4.

gorilla

5.

zigzag

6.

sponge

Phonics Intervention Centers
Variant Consonant and Vowel Sounds

EMC 3528 • © Evan-Moor Corp.

hard g

soft g

1. globe

2. giant

3. angel

4. gorilla

5. zigzag

6. sponge

Phonics Intervention Centers
Variant Consonant and Vowel Sounds

EMC 3528 • © Evan-Moor Corp.

hard **g**	soft **g**

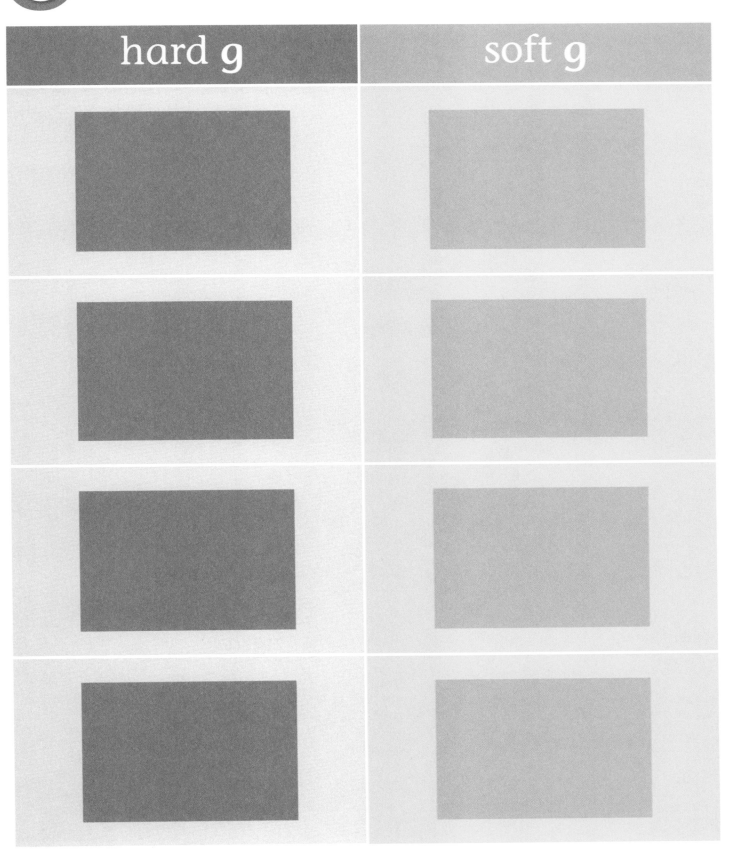

1. globe

2. giant

3. angel

4. gorilla

5. zigzag

6. sponge

hard g

soft g

1.  globe

2.  giant

3.  angel

4.  gorilla

5.  zigzag

6.  sponge

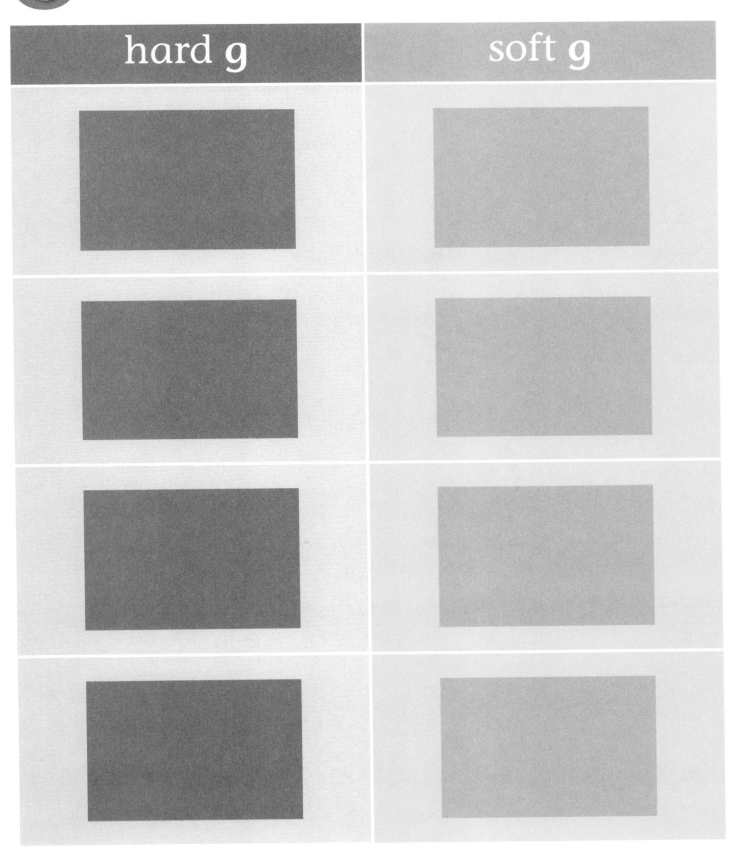

hard **g**

soft **g**

1.  globe

2.  giant

3.  angel

4.  gorilla

5. 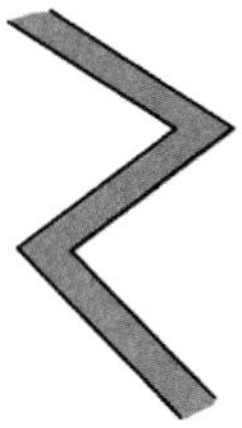 zigzag

6.  sponge

Student 2

giraffe

cage

gerbil

hinge

garden

goldfish

plug

organ

Student 1

giraffe

cage

gerbil

hinge

garden

goldfish

plug

organ

Student 2

EMC 3528 • Center 6 • Mat A

Student 2

EMC 3528 • Center 6 • Mat A

Student 2

EMC 3528 • Center 6 • Mat A

Student 2

EMC 3528 • Center 6 • Mat A

Student 2

EMC 3528 • Center 6 • Mat A

Student 2

EMC 3528 • Center 6 • Mat A

Student 2

EMC 3528 • Center 6 • Mat A

Student 1

EMC 3528 • Center 6 • Mat A

Student 1

EMC 3528 • Center 6 • Mat A

Student 2

EMC 3528 • Center 6 • Mat A

Student 1

EMC 3528 • Center 6 • Mat A

Student 1

EMC 3528 • Center 6 • Mat A

Student 2

EMC 3528 • Center 6 • Mat A

Student 1

EMC 3528 • Center 6 • Mat A

Student 1

EMC 3528 • Center 6 • Mat A

center
6

Student 4

giraffe

cage

gerbil

hinge

garden

goldfish

plug

organ

Student 3

giraffe

cage

gerbil

hinge

garden

goldfish

plug

organ

Student 4

EMC 3528 • Center 6 • Mat A

Student 4

EMC 3528 • Center 6 • Mat A

Student 4

EMC 3528 • Center 6 • Mat A

Student 4

EMC 3528 • Center 6 • Mat A

Student 3

EMC 3528 • Center 6 • Mat A

Student 3

EMC 3528 • Center 6 • Mat A

Student 3

EMC 3528 • Center 6 • Mat A

Student 3

EMC 3528 • Center 6 • Mat A

Student 4

EMC 3528 • Center 6 • Mat A

Student 4

EMC 3528 • Center 6 • Mat A

Student 3

EMC 3528 • Center 6 • Mat A

Student 3

EMC 3528 • Center 6 • Mat A

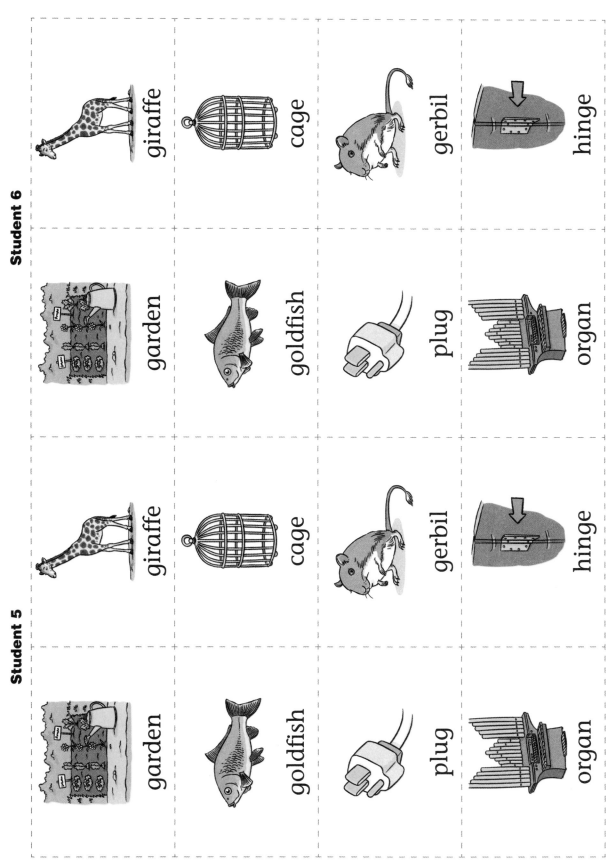

Student 6

giraffe

cage

gerbil

hinge

garden

goldfish

plug

organ

Student 5

giraffe

cage

gerbil

hinge

garden

goldfish

plug

organ

Student 6

EMC 3528 • Center 6 • Mat A

Student 6

EMC 3528 • Center 6 • Mat A

Student 6

EMC 3528 • Center 6 • Mat A

Student 6

EMC 3528 • Center 6 • Mat A

Student 6

EMC 3528 • Center 6 • Mat A

Student 6

EMC 3528 • Center 6 • Mat A

Student 6

EMC 3528 • Center 6 • Mat A

Student 5

EMC 3528 • Center 6 • Mat A

Student 5

EMC 3528 • Center 6 • Mat A

Student 5

EMC 3528 • Center 6 • Mat A

Student 5

EMC 3528 • Center 6 • Mat A

Student 5

EMC 3528 • Center 6 • Mat A

Student 5

EMC 3528 • Center 6 • Mat A

Student 5

EMC 3528 • Center 6 • Mat A

Student 1	Student 2	Student 3	Student 4	Student 5	Student 6
hard g	hard g	hard g	hard g	hard g	hard g
hard g	hard g	hard g	hard g	hard g	hard g
hard g	hard g	hard g	hard g	hard g	hard g
soft g	soft g	soft g	soft g	soft g	soft g
soft g	soft g	soft g	soft g	soft g	soft g
soft g	soft g	soft g	soft g	soft g	soft g

Student 6	Student 5	Student 4	Student 3	Student 2	Student 1
EMC 3528 Center 6 • Mat B	EMC 3528 Center 6 • Mat B	EMC 3528 Center 6 • Mat B	EMC 3528 Center 6 • Mat B	EMC 3528 Center 6 • Mat B	EMC 3528 Center 6 • Mat B
Student 6	Student 5	Student 4	Student 3	Student 2	Student 1
EMC 3528 Center 6 • Mat B	EMC 3528 Center 6 • Mat B	EMC 3528 Center 6 • Mat B	EMC 3528 Center 6 • Mat B	EMC 3528 Center 6 • Mat B	EMC 3528 Center 6 • Mat B
Student 6	Student 5	Student 4	Student 3	Student 2	Student 1
EMC 3528 Center 6 • Mat B	EMC 3528 Center 6 • Mat B	EMC 3528 Center 6 • Mat B	EMC 3528 Center 6 • Mat B	EMC 3528 Center 6 • Mat B	EMC 3528 Center 6 • Mat B
Student 6	Student 5	Student 4	Student 3	Student 2	Student 1
EMC 3528 Center 6 • Mat B	EMC 3528 Center 6 • Mat B	EMC 3528 Center 6 • Mat B	EMC 3528 Center 6 • Mat B	EMC 3528 Center 6 • Mat B	EMC 3528 Center 6 • Mat B

Name _____

Practice It!

Read the word.
Draw a line to the box that shows a word with the same sound of **g**.

1. gasp

2. goose

3. stage

game

4. angry

5. energy

6. ranger

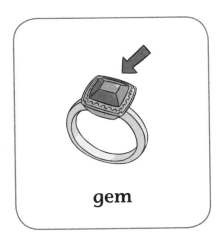

gem

7. wagon

8. legend

Read It!

Write the two words on the correct lines to complete each sentence.

1. (gets   grades)

Grace always _____ good _____.

2. (giant   giraffe)

A _____ is a _____ land animal.

3. (hungry   orange)

Ginny was _____, so she ate an _____.

4. (goose   larger)

A _____ is _____ than a duck.

5. (gem   gold)

The _____ in Grandma's _____ ring is huge.

6. (age   goldfish)

Gabe got his first _____ at the _____ of six.

7. (gear   ranger)

A park _____ found our lost camping _____.

8. (gulp   seagull)

Can a _____ eat a fish in one _____?

center

7

Two Sounds of s

For the Teacher

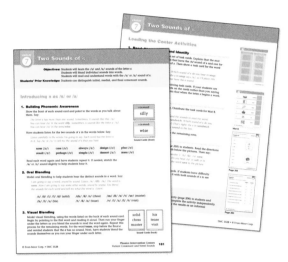

Lesson Plan

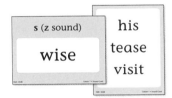

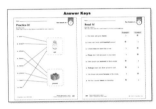

Sound Cards

Answer Keys

For the Student

front (Mat A)

back (Mat B)

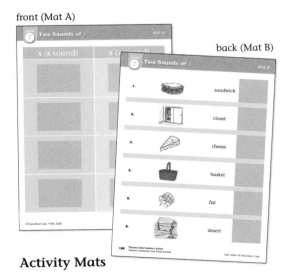

Activity Mats

Task Cards

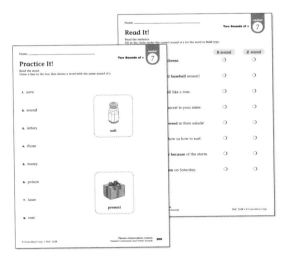

Practice and Assessment Activities

Two Sounds of s

Objectives: Students will learn the /s/ and /z/ sounds of the letter *s*.
Students will blend individual sounds into words.
Students will read and understand words with the /s/ or /z/ sound of *s*.

Students' Prior Knowledge: Students can distinguish initial, medial, and final consonant sounds.

Introducing s as /s/ or /z/

1. Building Phonemic Awareness

Show the front of each sound card and point to the words as you talk about them. Say:

*The letter **s** has more than one sound. Sometimes, it sounds like this: /s/.
You can hear /s/ in the word **silly**. Sometimes, **s** sounds like the letter **z**: /z/.
You can hear /z/ in the word **wise**.*

Have students listen for the two sounds of *s* in the words below. Say:

*Listen carefully to the words I'm going to say. Each word has the letter **s**
in it. Say /s/ or /z/ to tell me the sound of **s** that you hear.*

Sound Cards (front)

nose (/z/)	case (/s/)	always (/z/)	design (/z/)	plus (/s/)
result (/z/)	perhaps (/s/)	simple (/s/)	dessert (/z/)	mess (/s/)

Read each word again and have students repeat it. If needed, stretch the /s/ or /z/ sound slightly to help students hear it.

2. Oral Blending

Model oral blending to help students hear the distinct sounds in a word. Say:

*I am going to say a word, sound by sound. Listen: /s/ /ōō/ /n/. The word is
soon. Now I am going to say some other words, sound by sound. You blend
the sounds for each word and tell me what the word is. Listen:*

/s/ /ŏ/ /l/ /ĭ/ /d/ (solid)	/ch/ /ĕ/ /s/ (chess)	/m/ /ă/ /s/ /t/ /ur/ (master)
/h/ /ĭ/ /z/ (his)	/t/ /ē/ /z/ (tease)	/v/ /ĭ/ /z/ /ĭ/ /t/ (visit)

3. Visual Blending

Model visual blending, using the words listed on the back of each sound card. Begin by pointing to the first word and reading it aloud. Then run your finger under the letters as you blend the sounds to read the word again. Repeat this process for the remaining words. For the word **tease**, stop before the final *e* and remind students that the *e* has no sound. Next, have students blend the sounds themselves as you run your finger under each letter.

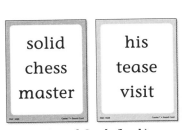

Sound Cards (back)

Leading the Center Activities

1. Read, Discriminate, and Identify

Give each student Mat A and a set of task cards. Explain that the mat has two columns: one for words that have the /s/ sound of s and one for words that have the /z/ sound of s. Then show a task card for the word **soap** and say:

> *The word on this card is **soap**. Which sound of s do you hear in **soap**: /s/ or /z/? (/s/) That's right; the s in **soap** says /s/, so I'll place this card in the column for words that have the s sound.*

Repeat this process with the remaining task cards. If your students are capable, have them read the words on the cards rather than you saying them. You may wish to tell students that when the letter s begins a word, the s says /s/.

2. Read and Understand

Have students turn over their mats. Distribute the task cards for Mat B. Then say:

> *Look at the word in row 1. Let's blend the sounds to read the word: /s/ /ă/ /n/ /d/ /w/ /ĭ/ /ch/ **sandwich**. Which sound of s do you hear in **sandwich**: /s/ or /z/? (/s/) That's right; the s in **sandwich** says /s/, so place a card that says **s sound** in the box.*

Repeat this process with the words in the remaining rows.

3. Practice the Skill

Distribute the Practice It! activity (page 205) to students. Read the directions aloud and have students read the words below the pictures. Then say:

> *Let's blend the sounds to read word number 1: /s/ /ā/ /v/ **save**. Do you hear /s/ or /z/ in **save**? (/s/) Do you hear /s/ in **salt** or in **present**? (salt) Now draw a line from the word **save** to the picture of the salt shaker.*

Repeat this process for the remaining words. If students have difficulty decoding a word, tell them to try saying it with both sounds of s to see which sound makes a familiar word.

Apply and Assess

After the lesson, distribute the Read It! activity (page 206) to students and read the directions aloud. Have students complete the activity independently. Then listen to them read the sentences. Use the results as an informal assessment of students' skill mastery.

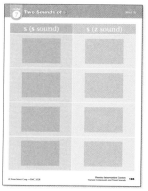

Mat A

Mat B

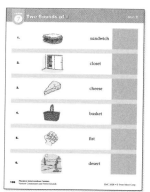

Page 205

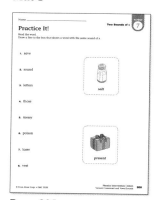

Page 206

s (s sound)

silly

s (z sound)

wise

EMC 3528

Answer Keys

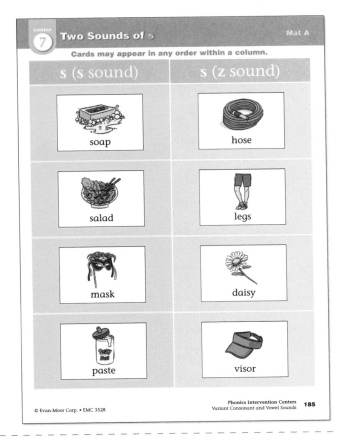

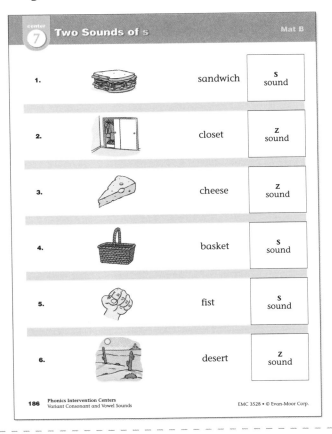

his
tease
visit

Center 7 • Sound Card

solid
chess
master

Center 7 • Sound Card

Answer Keys

Name _____

Practice It!

Read the word.
Draw a line to the box that shows a word with the same sound of *s*.

Two Sounds of *s*

center 7

1. save
2. sound
3. letters
4. those
5. messy
6. poison
7. laser
8. vest

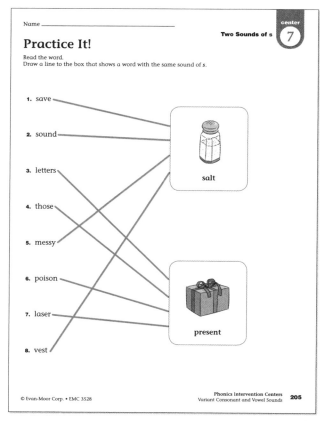

salt

present

Phonics Intervention Centers
Variant Consonant and Vowel Sounds **205**

Name _____

Read It!

Read the sentence.
Fill in the circle under the correct sound of *s* for the word in **bold** type.

Two Sounds of *s*

center 7

	S sound	**Z sound**
1. This farm sells goat **cheese**.	○	●
2. Casey can't wait until **baseball** season!	●	○
3. A daisy **does** not smell like a rose.	○	●
4. **Please** don't tell my secret to your sister.	○	●
5. Some people put **seaweed** in their salads!	●	○
6. **Perhaps** Jessie can show us how to surf.	●	○
7. Our house lost power **because** of the storm.	○	●
8. Sue has a music **lesson** on Saturday.	●	○

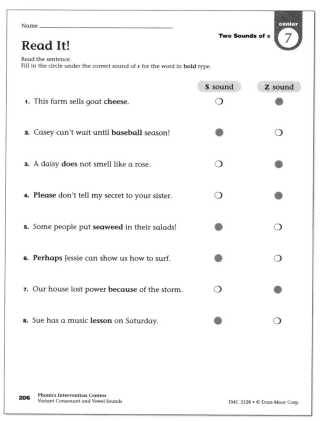

center 7 Two Sounds of s

Mat A

s (s sound)	s (z sound)

© Evan-Moor Corp. • EMC 3528

Phonics Intervention Centers
Variant Consonant and Vowel Sounds **185**

1.   sandwich

2.   closet

3.   cheese

4.   basket

5.   fist

6.   desert

s (s sound)	s (z sound)

1. sandwich

2. closet

3. cheese

4. basket

5. fist

6. desert

Phonics Intervention Centers
Variant Consonant and Vowel Sounds

s (s sound)

s (z sound)

1.  sandwich

2.  closet

3.  cheese

4.  basket

5. fist

6.  desert

s (s sound)	s (z sound)

1. sandwich

2. closet

3. cheese

4. basket

5. fist

6. desert

Phonics Intervention Centers
Variant Consonant and Vowel Sounds

EMC 3528 • © Evan-Moor Corp.

s (s sound)	s (z sound)

1. sandwich

2. closet

3. cheese

4. basket

5. fist

6. desert

Phonics Intervention Centers
Variant Consonant and Vowel Sounds

s (s sound)	s (z sound)

Two Sounds of s

1. sandwich

2. closet

3. cheese

4. basket

5. fist

6. desert

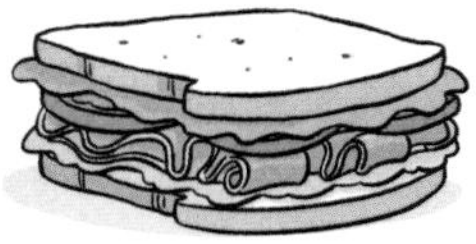

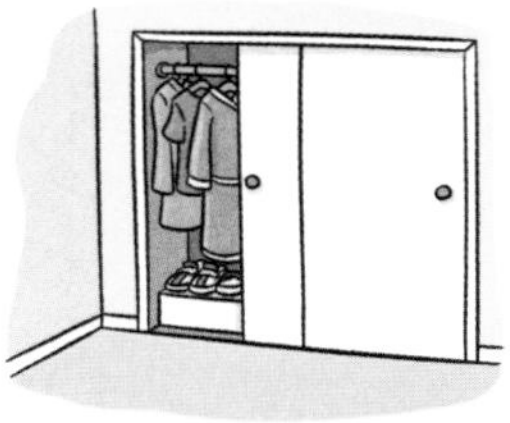

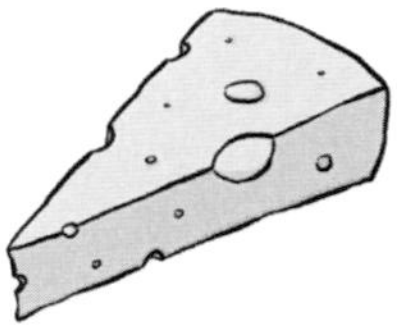

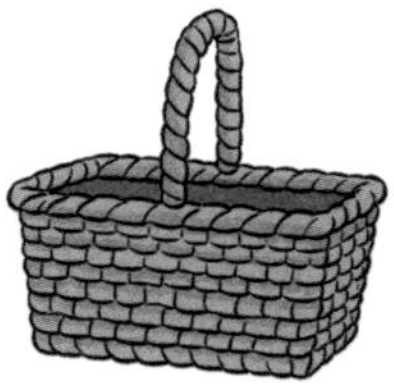

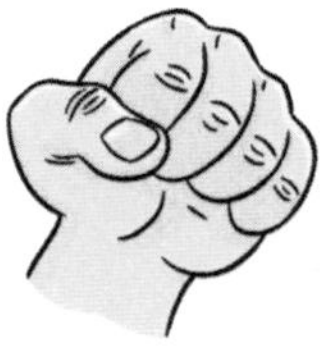

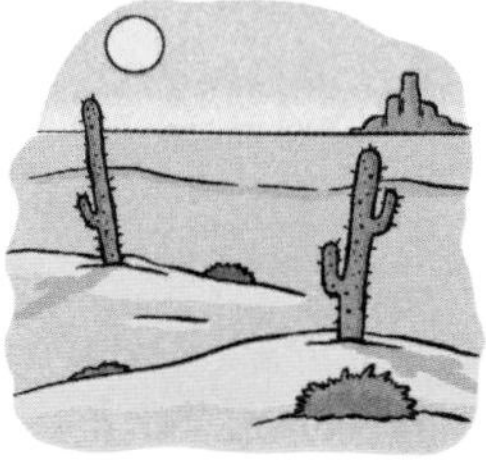

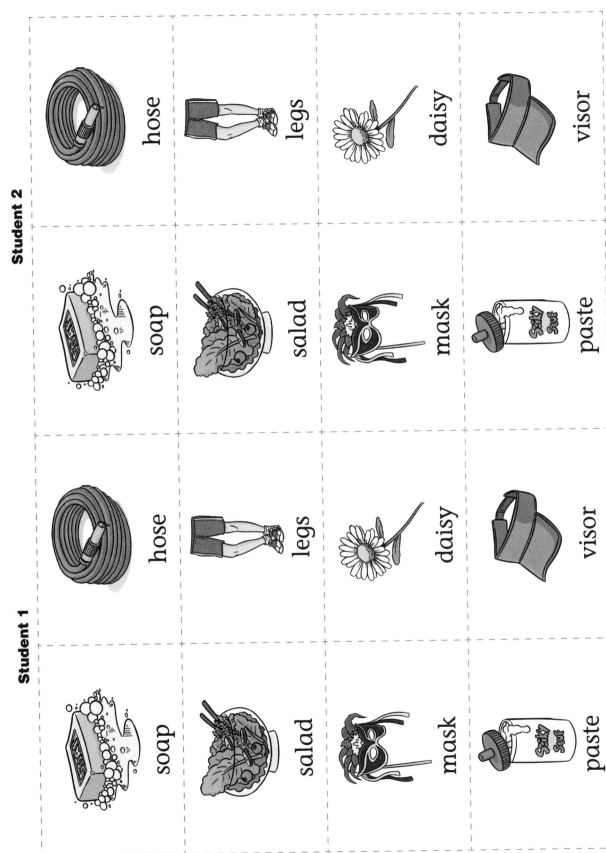

Student 2

hose

legs

daisy

visor

soap

salad

mask

paste

Student 1

hose

legs

daisy

visor

soap

salad

mask

paste

Student 2

EMC 3528 • Center 7 • Mat A

Student 2

EMC 3528 • Center 7 • Mat A

Student 2

EMC 3528 • Center 7 • Mat A

Student 2

EMC 3528 • Center 7 • Mat A

Student 2

EMC 3528 • Center 7 • Mat A

Student 2

EMC 3528 • Center 7 • Mat A

Student 1

EMC 3528 • Center 7 • Mat A

Student 1

EMC 3528 • Center 7 • Mat A

Student 1

EMC 3528 • Center 7 • Mat A

Student 1

EMC 3528 • Center 7 • Mat A

Student 1

EMC 3528 • Center 7 • Mat A

Student 1

EMC 3528 • Center 7 • Mat A

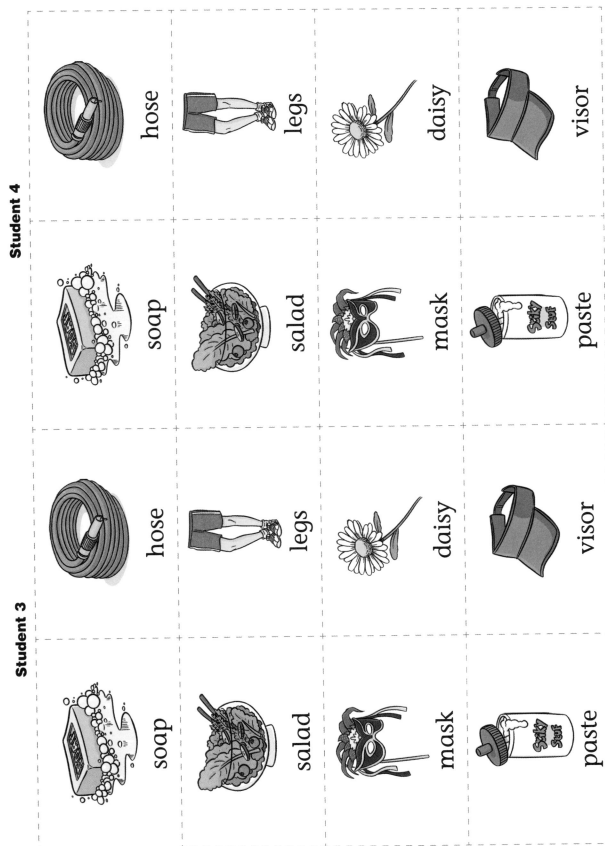

Student 4

hose

legs

daisy

visor

soap

salad

mask

paste

Student 3

hose

legs

daisy

visor

soap

salad

mask

paste

Student 4

EMC 3528 • Center 7 • Mat A

Student 4

EMC 3528 • Center 7 • Mat A

Student 4

EMC 3528 • Center 7 • Mat A

Student 4

EMC 3528 • Center 7 • Mat A

Student 4

EMC 3528 • Center 7 • Mat A

Student 4

EMC 3528 • Center 7 • Mat A

Student 4

EMC 3528 • Center 7 • Mat A

Student 4

EMC 3528 • Center 7 • Mat A

Student 3

EMC 3528 • Center 7 • Mat A

Student 3

EMC 3528 • Center 7 • Mat A

Student 3

EMC 3528 • Center 7 • Mat A

Student 3

EMC 3528 • Center 7 • Mat A

Student 3

EMC 3528 • Center 7 • Mat A

Student 3

EMC 3528 • Center 7 • Mat A

Student 3

EMC 3528 • Center 7 • Mat A

Student 3

EMC 3528 • Center 7 • Mat A

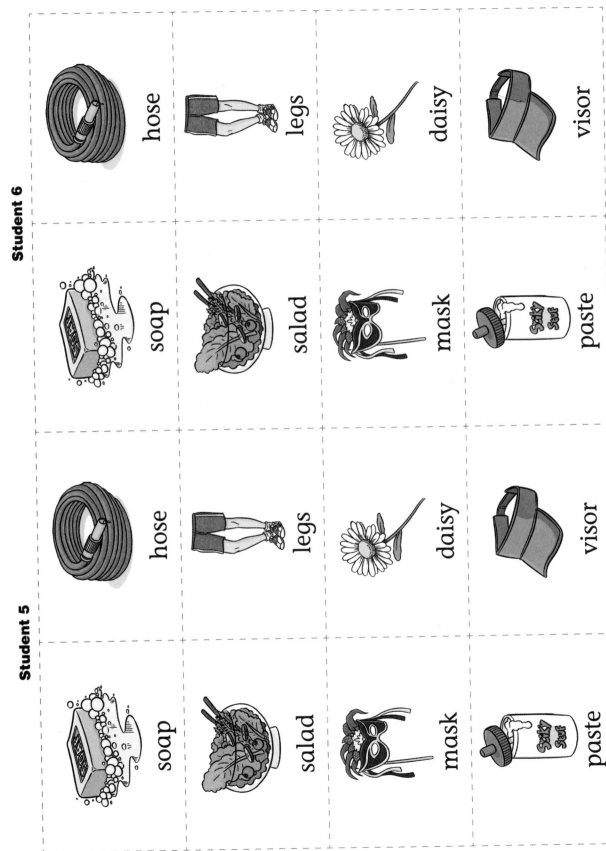

Student 6

hose

legs

daisy

visor

soap

salad

mask

paste

Student 5

hose

legs

daisy

visor

soap

salad

mask

paste

Student 6

EMC 3528 • Center 7 • Mat A

Student 6

EMC 3528 • Center 7 • Mat A

Student 6

EMC 3528 • Center 7 • Mat A

Student 6

EMC 3528 • Center 7 • Mat A

Student 6

EMC 3528 • Center 7 • Mat A

Student 6

EMC 3528 • Center 7 • Mat A

Student 6

EMC 3528 • Center 7 • Mat A

Student 6

EMC 3528 • Center 7 • Mat A

Student 5

EMC 3528 • Center 7 • Mat A

Student 5

EMC 3528 • Center 7 • Mat A

Student 5

EMC 3528 • Center 7 • Mat A

Student 5

EMC 3528 • Center 7 • Mat A

Student 5

EMC 3528 • Center 7 • Mat A

Student 5

EMC 3528 • Center 7 • Mat A

Student 5

EMC 3528 • Center 7 • Mat A

Student 5

EMC 3528 • Center 7 • Mat A

Student 1	Student 2	Student 3	Student 4	Student 5	Student 6
s sound	**s** sound	**s** sound	**s** sound	**s** sound	**s** sound
s sound	**s** sound	**s** sound	**s** sound	**s** sound	**s** sound
s sound	**s** sound	**s** sound	**s** sound	**s** sound	**s** sound
z sound	**z** sound	**z** sound	**z** sound	**z** sound	**z** sound
z sound	**z** sound	**z** sound	**z** sound	**z** sound	**z** sound
z sound	**z** sound	**z** sound	**z** sound	**z** sound	**z** sound

Task Cards

Student 6
EMC 3528
Center 7 • Mat B

Student 5
EMC 3528
Center 7 • Mat B

Student 4
EMC 3528
Center 7 • Mat B

Student 3
EMC 3528
Center 7 • Mat B

Student 2
EMC 3528
Center 7 • Mat B

Student 1
EMC 3528
Center 7 • Mat B

Student 6
EMC 3528
Center 7 • Mat B

Student 5
EMC 3528
Center 7 • Mat B

Student 4
EMC 3528
Center 7 • Mat B

Student 3
EMC 3528
Center 7 • Mat B

Student 2
EMC 3528
Center 7 • Mat B

Student 1
EMC 3528
Center 7 • Mat B

Student 6
EMC 3528
Center 7 • Mat B

Student 5
EMC 3528
Center 7 • Mat B

Student 4
EMC 3528
Center 7 • Mat B

Student 3
EMC 3528
Center 7 • Mat B

Student 2
EMC 3528
Center 7 • Mat B

Student 1
EMC 3528
Center 7 • Mat B

Student 6
EMC 3528
Center 7 • Mat B

Student 5
EMC 3528
Center 7 • Mat B

Student 4
EMC 3528
Center 7 • Mat B

Student 3
EMC 3528
Center 7 • Mat B

Student 2
EMC 3528
Center 7 • Mat B

Student 1
EMC 3528
Center 7 • Mat B

Student 6
EMC 3528
Center 7 • Mat B

Student 5
EMC 3528
Center 7 • Mat B

Student 4
EMC 3528
Center 7 • Mat B

Student 3
EMC 3528
Center 7 • Mat B

Student 2
EMC 3528
Center 7 • Mat B

Student 1
EMC 3528
Center 7 • Mat B

Student 6
EMC 3528
Center 7 • Mat B

Student 5
EMC 3528
Center 7 • Mat B

Student 4
EMC 3528
Center 7 • Mat B

Student 3
EMC 3528
Center 7 • Mat B

Student 2
EMC 3528
Center 7 • Mat B

Student 1
EMC 3528
Center 7 • Mat B

Practice It!

Read the word.
Draw a line to the box that shows a word with the same sound of *s*.

1. save

2. sound

3. letters

salt

4. those

5. messy

6. poison

present

7. laser

8. vest

Read It!

Read the sentence.
Fill in the circle under the correct sound of *s* for the word in **bold** type.

	S sound	**Z** sound
1. This farm sells goat **cheese**.	○	○
2. Casey can't wait until **baseball** season!	○	○
3. A daisy **does** not smell like a rose.	○	○
4. **Please** don't tell my secret to your sister.	○	○
5. Some people put **seaweed** in their salads!	○	○
6. **Perhaps** Jessie can show us how to surf.	○	○
7. Our house lost power **because** of the storm.	○	○
8. Sue has a music **lesson** on Saturday.	○	○

Consonant Sounds
Review c · g · s

For the Teacher

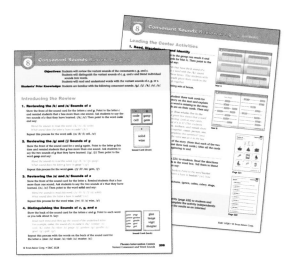

Lesson Plan

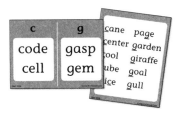

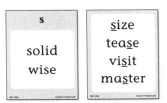

Sound Cards

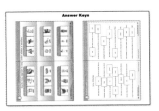

Answer Keys

For the Student

front (Mat A)

To make Mat A, place pages 214 and 215 side by side and laminate. (Turn over for Mat B.)

back (Mat B)

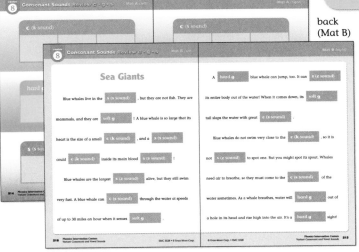

Activity Mats

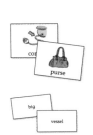

Task Cards

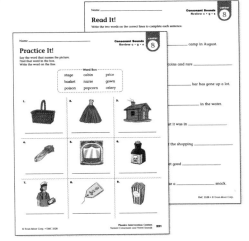

Practice and Assessment Activities

Phonics Intervention Centers
Variant Consonant and Vowel Sounds

Objectives: Students will review the variant sounds of the consonants *c*, *g*, and *s*.

Students will distinguish the variant sounds of *c*, *g*, and *s* and blend individual sounds into words.

Students will read and understand words with the variant sounds of *c*, *g*, or *s*.

Students' Prior Knowledge: Students are familiar with the following consonant sounds: /g/, /j/, /k/, /s/, /z/.

Introducing the Review

1. Reviewing the /k/ and /s/ Sounds of *c*

Show the front of the sound card for the letters *c* and *g*. Point to the letter *c* and remind students that *c* has more than one sound. Ask students to say the two sounds of *c* that they have learned. (/k/, /s/) Then point to the word **code** and say:

> *Blend the sounds to read this word.* (/k/ /ō/ /d/ code)
> *What sound does the letter c have in* **code**? (/k/)

Repeat this process for the word **cell**. (/s/ /ĕ/ /l/ cell, /s/)

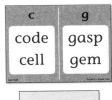

2. Reviewing the /g/ and /j/ Sounds of *g*

Show the front of the sound card for *c* and *g* again. Point to the letter *g* this time and remind students that *g* has more than one sound. Ask students to say the two sounds of *g* that they have learned. (/g/, /j/) Then point to the word **gasp** and say:

> *Blend the sounds to read this word.* (/g/ /ă/ /s/ /p/ gasp)
> *What sound does the letter g have in* **gasp**? (/g/)

Repeat this process for the word **gem**. (/j/ /ĕ/ /m/ gem, /j/)

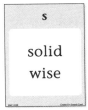

Sound Card (front)

3. Reviewing the /s/ and /z/ Sounds of *s*

Show the front of the sound card for the letter *s*. Remind students that *s* has more than one sound. Ask students to say the two sounds of *s* that they have learned. (/s/, /z/) Then point to the word **solid** and say:

> *Blend the sounds to read this word.* (/s/ /ŏ/ /l/ /ĭ/ /d/ solid)
> *What sound does the letter s have in* **solid**? (/s/)

Repeat this process for the word **wise**. (/w/ /ī/ /z/ wise, /z/)

4. Distinguishing the Sounds of *c*, *g*, and *s*

Show the back of the sound card for the letters *c* and *g*. Point to each word as you talk about it. Say:

> *Read each word and then say the sound of the underlined letter.*
> *For example,* **cane**: *the sound of c in* **cane** *is* /k/. (center: /s/; cool: /k/; cube: /k/; slice: /s/; page: /j/; garden: /g/; giraffe: /j/; goal: /g/; gull: /g/)

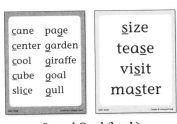

Sound Card (back)

Repeat this process with the words on the back of the sound card for the letter *s*. (size: /s/; tease: /z/; visit: /z/; master: /s/)

Leading the Center Activities

1. Read, Discriminate, and Identify ....

Place Mat A where all students in the group can reach it and give each student three task cards for Mat A. Then point to the first set of boxes on the mat and say:

*These green boxes are for words that have the **k** sound of **c**. Look at your cards. If you have a word with the /k/ sound in it, place the card in one of these boxes.* (The students with the words **camel**, **cord**, and **curb** place their cards in the boxes.) *Now let's read the words together.*

Repeat this process for the remaining sets of boxes.

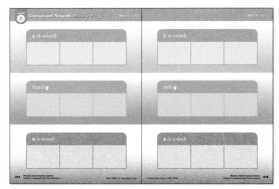

Mat A

2. Read and Understand ....

Turn over the mat and give each student three task cards for Mat B. Read aloud the title of the story on the mat and explain that each green box shows where a word is missing in the story. Tell students that the missing words are on their cards. Then say:

*Listen to me read the first sentence: **Blue whales live in the _____, but they are not fish.** The green box shows that a word with the **s** sound of the letter **s** is missing. Look at your cards. Who has a word with the /s/ sound of **s** in it?* (The students with the words **coast**, **person**, **sea**, **surface**, and **vessel** show their cards.) *Let's read these words together: **coast**, **person**, **sea**, **surface**, **vessel**. Which word best completes this sentence?* (sea) *That's right; so place the card with the word **sea** on it in the box.*

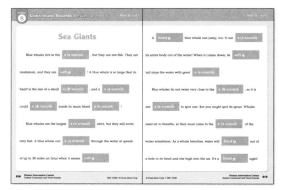

Mat B

Repeat this process for each sentence of the story. (Note that each of the two sounds of **c**, **g**, and **s** are used on at least three task cards.) After all the cards are on the mat, read the story from beginning to end.

3. Practice the Skill ....

Distribute the Practice It! activity (page 221) to students. Read the directions aloud and have students read the words in the word box. Tell them to blend the sounds as they read each word. Then say:

Look at the first picture. What is it? (a basket) *Point to the word **basket** in the word box. What sound does the letter **s** have in **basket**?* (/s/) *Now write the word **basket** under the picture.*

Repeat this process with the remaining pictures. (gown, cabin, celery, stage, poison, nurse, price, popcorn)

Page 221

Apply and Assess

After the lesson, distribute the Read It! activity (page 222) to students and read the directions aloud. Have students complete the activity independently. Then listen to them read the sentences. Use the results as an informal assessment of students' skill mastery.

Page 222

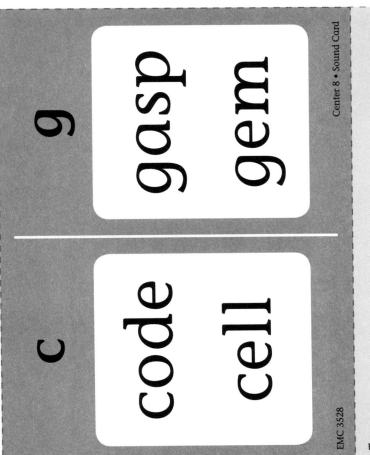

g

gasp

gem

c

code

cell

s

solid

wise

EMC 3528

Answer Keys

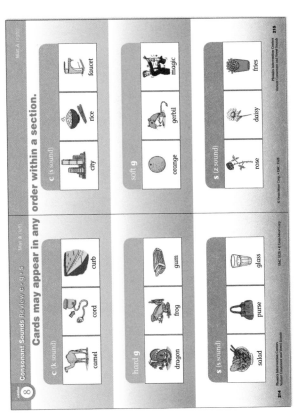

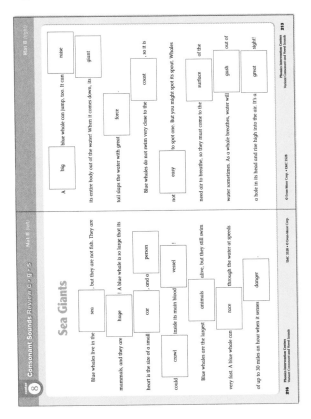

size

tea**s**e

vi**s**it

ma**s**ter

Center 8 • Sound Card

cane   pa**g**e

center   **g**arden

cool   **g**iraffe

cube   **g**oal

sli**c**e   **g**ull

Center 8 • Sound Card

Answer Keys

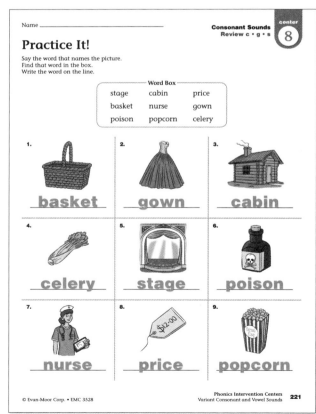

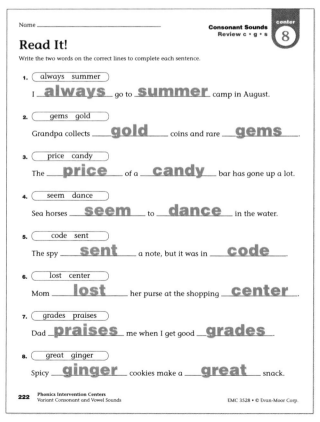

A [hard g] blue whale can jump, too. It can [s (z sound)]

its entire body out of the water! When it comes down, its [soft g]

tail slaps the water with great [c (s sound)] .

Blue whales do not swim very close to the [c (k sound)] , so it is

not [s (z sound)] to spot one. But you might spot its spout. Whales

need air to breathe, so they must come to the [c (s sound)] of the

water sometimes. As a whale breathes, water will [hard g] out of

a hole in its head and rise high into the air. It's a [hard g] sight!

c (**k** sound)

hard **g**

s (**s** sound)

c (s sound)

soft g

s (z sound)

Sea Giants

Blue whales live in the [s (s sound)] , but they are not fish. They are

mammals, and they are [soft g] ! A blue whale is so large that its

heart is the size of a small [c (k sound)] , and a [s (s sound)]

could [c (k sound)] inside its main blood [s (s sound)] !

Blue whales are the largest [s (z sound)] alive, but they still swim

very fast. A blue whale can [c (s sound)] through the water at speeds

of up to 30 miles an hour when it senses [soft g] .

camel

cord

curb

city

rice

faucet

dragon

frog

gum

orange

gerbil

magic

salad

purse

glass

rose

daisy

fries

EMC 3528 • Center 8 • Mat A   EMC 3528 • Center 8 • Mat A   EMC 3528 • Center 8 • Mat A

EMC 3528 • Center 8 • Mat A   EMC 3528 • Center 8 • Mat A   EMC 3528 • Center 8 • Mat A

EMC 3528 • Center 8 • Mat A   EMC 3528 • Center 8 • Mat A   EMC 3528 • Center 8 • Mat A

EMC 3528 • Center 8 • Mat A   EMC 3528 • Center 8 • Mat A   EMC 3528 • Center 8 • Mat A

EMC 3528 • Center 8 • Mat A   EMC 3528 • Center 8 • Mat A   EMC 3528 • Center 8 • Mat A

EMC 3528 • Center 8 • Mat A   EMC 3528 • Center 8 • Mat A   EMC 3528 • Center 8 • Mat A

animals	big	car
coast	crawl	danger
easy	force	giant
great	gush	huge
person	race	raise
sea	surface	vessel

EMC 3528
Center 8 • Mat B

EMC 3528
Center 8 • Mat B

EMC 3528
Center 8 • Mat B

EMC 3528
Center 8 • Mat B

EMC 3528
Center 8 • Mat B

EMC 3528
Center 8 • Mat B

EMC 3528
Center 8 • Mat B

EMC 3528
Center 8 • Mat B

EMC 3528
Center 8 • Mat B

EMC 3528
Center 8 • Mat B

EMC 3528
Center 8 • Mat B

EMC 3528
Center 8 • Mat B

EMC 3528
Center 8 • Mat B

EMC 3528
Center 8 • Mat B

EMC 3528
Center 8 • Mat B

EMC 3528
Center 8 • Mat B

EMC 3528
Center 8 • Mat B

EMC 3528
Center 8 • Mat B

Practice It!

Say the word that names the picture.
Find that word in the box.
Write the word on the line.

Word Box

stage	cabin	price
basket	nurse	gown
poison	popcorn	celery

1.

_____

2.

_____

3.

_____

4.

_____

5.

_____

6.

_____

7.

_____

8.

_____

9.

_____

Read It!

Write the two words on the correct lines to complete each sentence.

1. (always   summer)

I _____ go to _____ camp in August.

2. (gems   gold)

Grandpa collects _____ coins and rare _____.

3. (price   candy)

The _____ of a _____ bar has gone up a lot.

4. (seem   dance)

Sea horses _____ to _____ in the water.

5. (code   sent)

The spy _____ a note, but it was in _____.

6. (lost   center)

Mom _____ her purse at the shopping _____.

7. (grades   praises)

Dad _____ me when I get good _____.

8. (great   ginger)

Spicy _____ cookies make a _____ snack.

Enrich any core writing or language arts program!

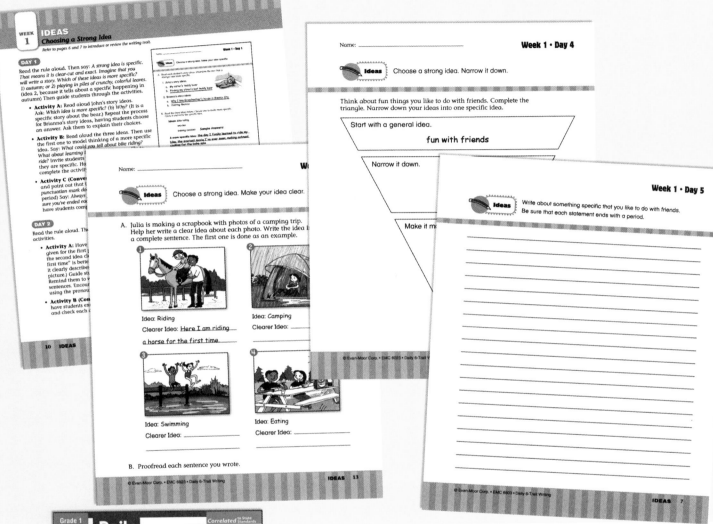

Daily 6-Trait Writing

Grade

1	EMC 6021
2	EMC 6022
3	EMC 6023
4	EMC 6024
5	EMC 6025
6+	EMC 6026

Features:

- 125 scaffolded, trait-based writing lessons

- A trait-based writing rubric

- Teacher pages that include an easy-to-follow teaching path and ideas for modeling and eliciting student responses

- Activities that cover narrative, expository, descriptive, and persuasive writing

Help build your child's language skills!

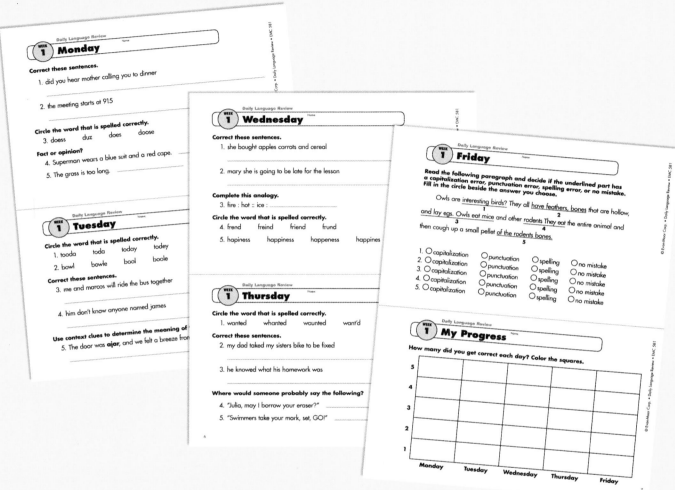

Repeated, focused practice in:

- sentence editing

- corrections in punctuation, capitalization, spelling, grammar, and vocabulary

- additional activities that cover a wide range of language and reading skills

Daily Language Review

Grade

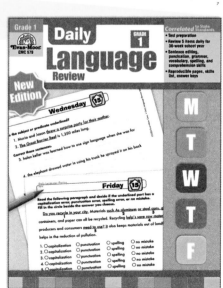